FOREWORD BY

The MIRACLE MORNING
for PARENTS & FAMILIES

How to Bring Out The Best In Your KIDS and Your SELF

Hal Elrod • Mike & Lindsay McCarthy

With Honorée Corder

THE MIRACLE MORNING FOR PARENTS & FAMILIES

Hal Elrod, Mike & Lindsay McCarthy
with Honorée Corder

Interior Design: Christina Culbertson, 3CsBooks.com

A Special Invitation from Hal

Fans and readers of *The Miracle Morning* make up an extraordinary community of like-minded individuals who wake up each day dedicated to fulfilling the unlimited potential that is within all of us. As the author of *The Miracle Morning*, it was my desire to create an online space where readers and fans could go to connect, get encouragement, share best practices, support one another, discuss the book, post videos, find an accountability partner, and even swap smoothie recipes and exercise routines.

I honestly had no idea that The Miracle Morning Community would become one of the most inspiring, engaged, and supportive online communities in the world, but it has. I'm blown away by the caliber of our 40,000+ members, which consists of people from all around the globe and is growing daily.

Just go to **www.MyTMMCommunity.com** and request to join The Miracle Morning Community (on Facebook). Here you'll be able to connect with others who are already practicing The Miracle Morning—many of whom have been doing it for years—to get additional support and accelerate your success. I'll be moderating the community and checking in regularly. I look forward to seeing you there!

If you'd like to connect with me personally on social media, follow **@HalElrod** on Twitter and **Facebook.com/YoPalHal** on Facebook. Please feel free to send me a direct message, leave a comment, or ask me a question. I do my best to answer every single one, so let's connect soon!

DEDICATION

HAL

This book is dedicated to my awesome parents, and my family.

To Mom, for dedicating your life to raising me and instilling the values of compassion, selflessness, hard work, and others that I'll do my best to share throughout this book.

To Dad, thank you for always believing in me, making life fun, and supporting my dreams. From starting my first DJ business at age 15, to selling Cutco knives, your support and your belief in me have always been unwavering.

To Ursula, my *wife-for-life*, you are always the first person I think of and feel grateful for during my Miracle Morning. Thank you so much for dedicating yourself to being the amazing mom that our kids deserve, dedicating time to improving yourself, and doing so much to support our family. You are the glue that holds the Elrod clan together, and I couldn't do what I do without you. I love you so much.

To Sophie & Halsten, being your dad is the greatest joy of my life! You are my two favorite humans on the planet, destined to make a huge, positive impact in the world, and I am committed to helping you to fulfill your potential and live the life of your dreams (while helping others to do the same, of course). I love you both more than I know how to put into words! :)

LINDSAY

This book is dedicated to my family. I am thankful for my own parents, for their love and support over the years, and for giving me both roots and wings. I love and appreciate my husband Mike for his undying support and gentle nudging to follow my passions. I am beyond grateful for Tyler as he was the inspiration behind this book. My sweet Ember has been my alarm clock, my teacher, and is now my accountability partner.

MIKE

This book is dedicated to not just my own parents, Jan and Rich, but to all the amazing parents out there who made a decision to step up and take full responsibility for the growth and safety of their children. My parents in particular supported me, and no matter what bad decisions I made, they always stuck by my side, loved me, and never gave up on me. I am also deeply grateful to my grandparents, Rich and Ruth McCarthy and Lee and Joe Baruzzi. They showered me with love and guidance for as long as they possibly could. I love and miss you all dearly. I would also like to thank my children, Tyler and Ember, for being the inspiration for this book and my beautiful wife, Lindsay, for everything she does to support our family, the way she loves me unconditionally, and her undeniable dedication to helping our children flourish at the highest levels. This book was her idea, and she has worked tirelessly on this project. I am so proud of the courage and strength she has shown. I love you Lindsay!

CONTENTS

FOREWORD
By Jim Sheils

A mentor of mine once told me, "Set your life to consistent rhythms—it's the only way to freedom."

At first, this made no sense. I had thought the opposite. I thought that if I kept consistent rhythms, I would lose freedom. I would be less effective. I would lose excitement and adventure. I would even dull my overall meaning and purpose. After all, doing the same thing over and over just gets boring and ineffective, right?

Wrong.

I was 100 percent wrong. In fact, effective rhythms (which are powerful habits that are consistently practiced in our lives) are the very fuel of success and a life of deeper meaning. In all my studies and experiences, it's the people who consistently rhythmize their lives who become the most successful and fulfilled—not only in their professional lives, but also in their home lives as well. The problem is truly great rhythms that improve family are rare—especially ones that involve our children.

This is the very reason I wrote *The Family Board Meeting*. I wanted to share a rhythm that would be engaging, inspiring, and effective for families worldwide, including children. I had seen the results that the practice had in my relationships with my children and wanted others to experience the same connection.

One of my closest friends, Pete Kuc, introduced me to Mike and Lindsay McCarthy while enjoying a casual day at the beach with my family. Immediately a friendship was born based around our core values: a love of family and a strong desire to improve education for our children. We all agreed on the importance of rhythms and the use of personal development for our children's growth.

It was obvious that Mike and Lindsay came from the same place of giving. They had gone deep into their Miracle Morning practice and created adaptations, along with Hal, to better involve their children. They were having great success in doing so. My wife and I quickly became their students.

Although Hal and I had met while speaking at different events, it's safe to say, neither of us were using each other's strategies. It was Mike and Lindsay, being the connectors they are, who gave each of us the nudge to check out one another's work and put our respective rhythms into practice. So glad it happened!

Sitting here today, I am not only a huge advocate of the Miracle Morning, but also my family was an early test case for putting the strategies of *The Miracle Morning for Parents and Families* in effect. We did a 45-day challenge with our children using the tools in this book. Each day we saw more depth and more connection to ourselves and each other, along with an overall greater sense of balance.

Mike, Lindsay, and Hal have written a road map for you and your children. If you can improve the start of every day, you can change the trajectory of your life.

Raising a family can be a tough job. We face a new world of technology, social issues, and challenges. Our kids face struggles none of us could have even imagined as children. One question is always playing in our heads: How do we support our children while improving the relationship we have with them?

I remember reading that Napoleon Hill said something along lines of "The most important education prepares us for the practical affairs of life." Unfortunately, this is not always the priority in our education system today. As parents, it's our job to fill these gaps and get our children the very best education supporting that important goal.

I believe *The Miracle Morning for Parents and Families* holds the key to success in this.

There are two reasons I believe in this book:

First, I have already implemented C.H.A.R.M.S. in my own family life and have seen the results. I have experienced connection and seen an increase of confidence and gratitude in my children and our family as a whole.

Second, I know for a fact that the authors of this book—Mike, Lindsay and Hal—are inspiring and authentic even "behind the curtain." Too many self-help gurus out there are like the Great and Powerful Oz. They portray a grand appearance on stage, yet behind the scenes, they're meek, empty, and disconnected. I have become very particular with accepting advice and guidance from people who present one image and live another. Especially when it comes to family life. Mike, Lindsay, and Hal are the real deal. *The Miracle Morning for Parents and Families* is the real deal. With real results.

Not all rhythms and advice out there are inspiring, effective, and enduring. On rare occasion, there is a rhythm that truly sticks and lives up to its claims. *The Miracle Morning for Parents and Families* will help you find one that works for you.

With Gratitude,

Jim Sheils

Lindsay's Introduction

It's not only children who grow. Parents do too. As much as we watch to see what our children do with their lives, they are watching us to see what we do with ours. I can't tell my children to reach for the sun. All I can do is reach for it, myself.
—Joyce Maynard, American novelist and journalist

I used to wake to the sound of little feet thundering into our bedroom as our daughter, Ember, climbed up on our bed and started to lift my eyelids saying, "Mommy, are you awake?" Once we got out of bed, we'd rush to eat, rush to get dressed, rush to get our things in the car, and then rush to the bus stop. When my son, Tyler, was safely on the bus to school, I'd spend the day picking up after my daughter, cleaning up each new mess only to turn around and find a new one. Whole weeks would pass while I visited the grocery store, attended Mommy and Me classes, and tried to make a dent in the mountain of laundry. I wasn't productive or organized. I simply ran from one thing to the next with no time to take a breath. I was surviving, but certainly not thriving.

I was on autopilot, going through the motions of life, following the path laid out for me by society. Together, Mike, our children, and I were the picture perfect wealthy family. Successful businessman husband, stay-at-home mom, and two children, an older boy and a younger girl. We lived in a big house on a hill overlooking a picturesque meadow and river. The perfect, happy family. But were we?

I did not wake up with excitement like Ember did. She couldn't wait to start her days chasing butterflies and building with blocks, but I had a hard time dragging myself out of bed. Something was definitely wrong with this picture.

I looked for answers, but nothing really changed for our family until I heard Hal Elrod speak about *The Miracle Morning* and his unique combination of daily morning practices called the Life S.A.V.E.R.S. I had been practicing meditation and journaling for years, but not always in the morning and not consistently. Hearing Hal's story of overcoming depression and coming back from nothing was so inspiring I decided to try it. I'd start my own Miracle Morning practice and incorporate the Life S.A.V.E.R.S. into my life.

Mike and I heard Hal speak at the 1Life Fully Lived Conference (www.1LifeFullyLived.org) in Reno, Nevada, in October 2014, and I read the entire book on the flight home. We committed to doing the Miracle Morning together and never looked back. After we'd been practicing for some time, the kids would come into our meditation room in the mornings and ask what we were doing. We explained that we were doing our Life S.A.V.E.R.S. and decided to teach the kids about them. Then they started doing them with us. It became an essential family activity to start our day.

Fast forward to the 2015 1Life Fully Lived West Coast Conference in Sacramento, California. Hal was again the headliner, but this time, I, too, was a presenter! The founder, Tim Rhode, who is a good friend of ours, had noticed my growth. Tim recognizes and give opportunities to people who have grown as a result of the work the nonprofit does, so he asked me if I would lead a breakout session on vision boards (an offer I couldn't refuse).

At the welcome reception for the presenters, I met Hal. I told him that I had been teaching our kids the Life S.A.V.E.R.S. and that the Miracle Morning was having a huge impact on our family. He was thrilled! I mentioned that our son was in California with us and would like to show Hal his affirmation book. At breakfast the next day, Tyler proudly recited his affirmations for Hal, who joyfully signed his book. Hal asked Tyler if he wanted to be featured in a new Miracle Morning book. Tyler was so excited he jumped up and down saying,

"Yes, yes, yes!" And Hal asked Mike and me if we would be interested in talking more about writing a book together.

A few days later, I woke up in the middle of the night with an idea to write a kids book using poems for each of the Life S.A.V.E.R.S. I headed to my computer and started typing. What came out were haikus, one for each of the Life S.A.V.E.R.S., along with exercises for kids to do with their parents. I shared it with Mike to see what his thoughts were, and he said he would forward it to Hal. Hal responded the next day to see if we'd be interested in coauthoring a book in his series, to which we obviously said, "Yes!" Little did Tyler know that when Hal offered to include him in the new book, his parents would be co-authoring it!

I won't say we are never rushed for time in the morning anymore, but for the most part, we are much happier. Now, when Ember comes into our bedroom in the morning, we are not usually asleep. Instead, we greet her with a smile and a hug. It's a much nicer way to start the day than having my eyelids stretched. Not only has the Miracle Morning led to more peaceful mornings, but I have also found courage and purpose in my life. I have become a better person and, because of that, a better parent. Doing the Life S.A.V.E.R.S. before my kids wake from their slumber has allowed me to fully secure my own oxygen mask before assisting them.

As a result of doing the Miracle Morning, I gained the courage to find a school for Tyler that allows us to live the life of our dreams. I also gained the confidence to write this book. I ran a half marathon while raising over $1000 for Tyler's school and have become a big supporter of 1Life Fully Lived as a presenter. Mike and I supported Tim by playing a large role (both financially and as Tim would say, "by getting butts in seats") in bringing the 1Life Fully Lived Personal Development Seminar to the East Coast. My favorite thing has been teaching my kids the Miracle Morning and collaborating with them to make it more kid friendly.

In this book, we will teach you the importance of having a morning practice and give you a step-by-step approach to getting out of bed. We will also show you what to do for the first hour once you get out of bed. Then we will dive into three not-so-obvious parenting principles. The first, Self-Leadership, is all about being a great role model for your kids. Energy Engineering will teach you how to stay on top of your self-care to help you be a step ahead of your offspring. Unwavering Focus is about becoming effective by increasing your efficiency. Lastly, we will introduce you to the three P's of exceptional parenting: Purposefulness, Playfulness, and Perspective.

I am not claiming to be a parenting *guru*, and this book is not going to hold you to an ideal of being a perfect parent, but it will guide you to find yourself again and be a great role model and parent for your kids. Within these pages, you'll learn how to introduce the Miracle Morning to your kids, and I'll offer some suggestions on how to adapt your own Miracle Morning when your kids don't cooperate.

To make it easier to share the principles and tell the stories in the book, it's been framed from my point of view. Mike and Hal are still with us on every page, but I'll be your official guide (except for Mike's Introduction) as we help you change your mornings and your life.

Before chapters three through ten, we've included profiles and parenting tips from some of the wisest and most effective parents we know. They also happen to be successful in other areas of their lives. We don't think it's a coincidence that these parents start their days with a Miracle Morning routine. Use these exceptional parents as your role models, as we do, to create your personal morning ritual. But remember, what works for them might not work for you. Every family must make decisions based on their needs, beliefs, and values.

If you're ready to have some *me* time every morning and greet your kids with a smiling face instead of chaos, then you've picked up the right book.

Lindsay McCarthy

Mike's Introduction

If we did all the things we are really capable of doing, we would literally astound ourselves.
—Thomas Edison, American inventor and businessman

I have done two things to massively change the trajectory of my life and shape the person I am today. The first was becoming a parent, and the second was starting my Miracle Morning practice. Nothing has inspired and equipped me to become a better person in every possible way.

I believe that one of the greatest journeys we can ever take is to become a parent. Nothing is more important than co-creating mini humans (aka children), loving them, and equipping them with the tools to grow and flourish so that they can develop and share their own unique gifts in the world. I always knew I wanted to be a father, but exactly why I wanted that was never clear to me—until I had my first child. Even then, it didn't happen overnight. Every day I embraced the role of father more and more. My life took on new meaning, bringing me a deep sense of clarity.

I learned how to dance with my fear instead of being overcome by it, and a new person emerged. I traded in and reprioritized my ego identities and upgraded the person I was being in the world. I started living for more than just myself. I became a father who happened to be a serial entrepreneur, leader, coach, trainer, husband, son, and now author. But what became perfectly clear to me was that I was a father first before any of those other identities. This transformation was not without its struggles, and at times I lost myself in the process. As it turns out, that was a good thing for me because it's also where I found my true self. Parenting and practicing the Life S.A.V.E.R.S. have changed me into the person I am today, and they continue to shape the person I will be tomorrow. Because I am a parent, I am fully committed to becoming the best version of myself and making a positive impact in the world.

It became very clear to me that a world that includes my children must be improved and healed, and I absolutely have to do my part to that end. At times, I feel like I have the weight of the world on my shoulders, and then I realize that I will happily bear that weight if it means a better life for my family—and every family for that matter. I don't take this lightly, because when we all make positive change together, the world in which our children live becomes the best version of itself. It becomes a healthy, happy, and harmonious place to live and grow.

I know that I am not alone on this journey; many other parents, like you, courageously take steps in their own development so they can make a big difference in the world for their children and their children's children. These parents inspire me on a daily basis, and many of them have contributed their stories to this book, sharing their struggles and knowledge with Lindsay and me. I truly believe that, as a species, we are waking up to the fact that we need to be the heroes of our own lives. As Mahatma Gandhi said, "Be the change you wish to see in the world." We are.

We have the opportunity to change the entire world for the better in just one generation. As our children watch us, they learn how they too can become the people they need to be to make a difference in the world. It starts with what we teach our children at home. I can think of no better way to shift the consciousness of our planet than to teach our children to get up every day and shape the person they are.

The Miracle Morning will transform anyone who follows the recipe, and that's a fact. So if the Miracle Morning has the power to transform any individual life, what kind of impact could it have on your children or in the life of your family? How would committing to this simple daily practice as a family positively impact you and the world at large? When I think about families doing the Life S.A.V.E.R.S. together across the globe, I get inspired about the world that we are co-creating together.

Imagine for a minute a world where supporting and encouraging each other was business as usual. Practicing the Life S.A.V.E.R.S. and teaching others how to win their mornings is the surprisingly simple tool to make this happen. In this new normal, being vulnerable, authentic, and compassionate will be valued and appreciated more than our worldly possessions, accomplishments, or the size of our bank accounts and homes. Once we focus on developing ourselves fully, *everything else* naturally follows suit and upgrades as well.

I want to commend you for picking up this book and taking a stand for the greatness that is inside of you and your children.

By the way, I am not an expert parent, and I probably won't win any parenting awards either, but I strive to be consciously incompetent as a parent and a human. What this means is that I simply want to acknowledge that I don't know it all and that there is always more to know about life and parenting. You aren't going to master yourself and parenting overnight. In fact, it will most likely take you a lifetime to truly master anything. However, if you get up every morning and chip away at it, you will be surprised to see how fast your life expands.

The same way a river carves a canyon, you too can become someone who lives life to the fullest. It doesn't happen in a day, it happens daily. As a successful business owner and leader, I have found no greater tool to improve my ability to lead than by practicing the Miracle Morning. It gives you the tools you need to start leading yourself more effectively. Once you can lead yourself in a purposeful way, you become a better leader to others. Then you are able to be a leader for your family or in the workplace. I hope your journey to discover your own limitless potential is filled with the awareness of how truly qualified and worthy you are to have an abundant life. I believe in you, even if you don't believe in yourself—yet.

We all have special gifts and talents that we must work to unlock and share with others in this lifetime. Reading this book and committing to the Life S.A.V.E.R.S. practice is the next logical step to make that happen. Godspeed, vaya con Dios, and carpe diem!

Mike McCarthy

— 1 —
WHY MORNINGS MATTER
(MORE THAN YOU THINK)

If John Lennon was right that life is what happens when you're making other plans, parenthood is what happens when everything is flipped over and spilling everywhere and you can't find a towel or a sponge or your "inside" voice.

—Kelly Corrigan, *Lift*

"The award for 'NOT being a Morning Person' goes to Lindsay." Yes, on my seventh grade overnight field trip, my bunkmates chose this one for me. Apparently it was so obvious I hated mornings that it defined me. If you told me then that I would one day write a book with my husband, encouraging people to wake up early to become a better person, I probably would have told you that you were crazy. But here we are!

Do you start your day feeling overwhelmed? I'd be willing to bet that most parents do. In fact, many don't even set an alarm clock. Their day starts when the kids run into the room, full of energy, feeling hungry, and in need of attention.

What if you could have that hour of peace and quiet you've been dreaming about? That clean, uncluttered mental space where you could regain your sense of elegance and dignity, where you're in total control and can proceed in an orderly, self-nurturing fashion? But you know you can't—or maybe you can but not today. Maybe when the kids start school or go off to college.

It's no wonder most parents start their days with procrastination, letting the kids set the agenda, and sending a message to their subconscious that says they don't have enough energy, or even the will to get out of bed. They think today will be another free-for-all where their personal goals and goals for the children go out the window in the usual scramble to meet the kids' immediate needs. After all, you can't debate about who comes first. Kids always are your first priority, right?

Add to this the fact that most people believe they aren't early risers, and the pattern of procrastination shows up early in life.

But what if you could change it?

What if, when the alarm clock starts beeping in the morning, you could consider it to be life's first gift? It's the gift of time that you can dedicate to becoming the person you need to be to achieve all of your goals and dreams—for yourself and your children—while the rest of the world is still asleep.

You might be thinking, *All of this sounds great, Lindsay. But. I. Am. Not. A. Morning. Person.*

I understand. I really do! You're not saying anything I haven't told myself a thousand times before. And believe me, I tried—and failed—many times to take control of our mornings. But that was before I discovered *The Miracle Morning.*

Stay with me here. In addition to wanting to raise the next Peyton Manning, I bet you also want to stop struggling and worrying about having more month than money, quit missing your goals, and release the intense and not-so-great emotions that go along with those challenges. These things get in the way of being an effective parent because they affect your self-esteem and prevent you from feeling good about yourself and your life.

I'm a firm believer in the advice given at the start of every airplane flight: Put your oxygen mask on first and then help your child. You won't be able to help anyone if you pass out due to lack of oxygen.

Many parents don't see this simple truth. They think that love means putting your own needs last, and they have so much to do that they never get to those needs. Over time, they end up exhausted, depressed, resentful, and overwhelmed.

Sound familiar?

Then know this:

Mornings are the key to all of it.

More important than even the *time* that you start your day is the *mindset* with which you start your day.

Although there's a chance you're reading this book after years of being a parent, there's also a good chance that you're reading this book in the early stages of your parenting journey, which means that you may be feeling overwhelmed and looking for answers. If that's the case, then learning to practice your Miracle Morning while the kids are still asleep is important to make sure you get your time, uninterrupted. The good news is … it's worth it, and it is far more fun and rewarding than you might expect.

But, before I get into exactly *how* you can master your mornings, let me make the case for *why*. Because, believe me, once you've uncovered the profound truth about mornings, you'll never want to miss one again.

Why Mornings Matter So Much

The more you dig into mornings, the more the proof mounts that the early bird gets *a lot* more than the worm. Here are just a few of the key advantages to giving up that last hour of sleep.

You'll be more proactive. Christoph Randler is a professor of biology at the University of Education in Heidelberg, Germany. In the July 2010 issue of *Harvard Business Review*, Randler found that "People whose performance peaks in the morning are better positioned for career success, because they're more proactive than people who are at their best in the evening." If there was ever a *career* in which being proactive is crucial to success, it's parenting. As parents, it's important for us to set the stage for the day so we can create a calm environment for our children.

You'll anticipate problems and head them off at the pass. Randler went on to surmise that morning people hold all of the important cards. They are "better able to anticipate and minimize problems, are proactive, have greater professional success and ultimately make higher wages." He noted that morning people are able to anticipate problems and handle them with grace and ease. If you think about it, this could be the key to decreasing the level of stress that inevitably comes with adding little ones to your household.

You'll plan like a pro. Planning is very important to exceptional parenting. It's been said that *when we fail to plan, we are indirectly planning to fail.* Morning folks have the time to organize, anticipate, and prepare for their day. Our sleepy counterparts are reactive, leaving a lot to chance. Aren't you more stressed when you sleep through your alarm? Getting up with the sun (or before) lets you jump-start your day. While everyone else is running around trying (and failing) to get their day under control, you'll be more calm, cool, and collected.

You'll have more energy. One component of your new Miracle Mornings will be morning exercise, which often is something neglected by busy parents. Yet, in as little as a few minutes, exercise sets a positive tone for the day. Increased blood to the brain will help you think more clearly and focus on what's most important. Fresh oxygen will permeate every cell in your body and increase your energy, which is why parents who exercise are in a better mood and in better shape, getting better sleep, and being more productive.

You'll gain early bird attitude advantages. Recently, researchers at the University of Barcelona in Spain, compared morning people, those early birds who like to get up at dawn, with evening people, night owls who prefer to stay up late and sleep in. Among the differences, they found that morning people tend to be more persistent and resistant to fatigue, frustration, and difficulties. That translates into lower levels of anxiety, rates of depression, and likelihood of substance abuse but higher life satisfaction. Sounds good to me! A better attitude has helped Mike and I create a more powerful mindset, which has made us better leaders for our family—and has helped us be more united in our roles as mother and father.

The evidence is in, and the experts have had their say. *Mornings contain the secret to an extraordinarily successful family life.*

Mornings? Really?

I admit it. To go from *I'm not a morning person* to *I really want to become a morning person* to *I'm up early every morning, and it's pretty darn amazing!* is a process. But after some trial and error, you will discover how to outfox, preempt, and foil your inner late sleeper so you can make early rising a habit. Okay, sounds great in theory, but you might be shaking your head and telling yourself, *There's no way. I'm already cramming 27 hours of stuff into 24 hours. How on earth could I get up an hour earlier than I already do?*

I ask the question, "How can you not?"

The key thing to understand is that the Miracle Morning isn't about denying yourself another hour of sleep so you can have an even longer, harder day. It's not even about waking up earlier. It's about waking up *better*.

Thousands of people around the planet are already living their own Miracle Mornings. Many of them were night owls. But they're making it work. In fact, they're *thriving*. And it's not because they simply added an hour to their day. It's because they added *the right* hour. And so can you.

Still skeptical? Then let me tell you this: *The hardest part about getting up an hour earlier is the first five minutes.* That's the crucial time when, tucked into your warm bed, you make the decision to start your day or hit the snooze button *just one more time*. It's the moment of truth, and the decision you make right then will change your day, your success, and your life.

And that's why the first five minutes is the starting point for *The Miracle Morning for Parents and Families*. It's time for you to win every morning! When we parents win our mornings, our children learn to do the same.

In the next two chapters, I'll make waking up early easier and more exciting than it's ever been in your life (even if you've *never* considered yourself to be a morning person), and we'll show you how to maximize those newfound morning minutes.

Chapters 4, 5, and 6 will reveal not-so-obvious parenting principles related to accelerating your personal growth, why you need to structure your life to gain endless amounts of energy, and how to optimize your ability to stay focused on your goals and what matters most.

Finally, chapters 7, 8, and 9 cover the critical skills you must master to become an exceptional parent. There's even a final bonus chapter from Hal that we think you are going to love!

We have a lot of ground to cover in this book, so let's jump right in.

— 2 —
IT ONLY TAKES FIVE MINUTES TO BECOME A MORNING PERSON

If you really think about it, hitting the snooze button in the morning doesn't even make sense. It's like saying, 'I hate getting up in the morning, so I do it over, and over, and over again.'
—Demetri Martin, Stand-Up Comedian

I t is possible to love waking up—even if you've *never* been a morning person.

I know you might not believe it. Right now you might think, *that might be true for early birds, but trust me, I've tried. I'm just not a morning person.*

But it's true. I know because I've been there. I used to let the kids wake me up, sleeping until the last possible moment, when they came tumbling into the room. And even then, it took me a while to get out of bed. The kids were like an alarm I simply couldn't turn off. I was a "snooze-aholic" as Hal calls them. I dreaded mornings. I hated waking up.

And now I love it.

How did I do it? When people ask me how I transformed myself into a morning person—and transformed my life in the process—I tell them I did it in five simple steps, one at a time. I know it may seem downright impossible. But take it from a former snooze-aholic: you can do this. And you can do it the same way I did.

That's the critical message about waking up—it's possible to change. Morning people aren't born—they're self-made. You can do it, and it doesn't require the willpower of an Olympic marathoner. I contend that when early rising becomes not only something you do, but *who you are* you will truly love mornings. Waking up will become for you like it is for me—effortless.

Not convinced? Suspend your disbelief a little and let me introduce you to the five-step process that changed my life. Five simple, snooze-proof keys that made waking up in the morning—even early in the morning—easier than ever before. Without this strategy, I would still be sleeping (or snoozing) through the alarm(s) each morning. Worse, I would still be clinging to the limiting belief that I am not a morning person.

And I would have missed a whole world of opportunity.

The Challenge with Waking Up

Waking up earlier is a bit like potty training: It's easy to get pumped up about all the diapers you're not going to have to change. But you quickly realize that potty training isn't easy. You have to go through the "accident" phase, which is a lot more hands on than the diapers. After a few days of it, you're seriously discouraged.

Well, we all know what happens then. Good intentions fly out the window, diapers go back on the kid, and we rationalize that they are not ready (and you may be right). It's easier to say, "Maybe tomorrow will be a better day to start," and then tomorrow turns into next week, next month, or even next year.

Mornings are not so different. Right now, you might be plenty motivated. But what happens tomorrow morning when that alarm goes off? How motivated will you be when you're yanked out of a deep sleep in a warm bed by a screaming alarm clock (or child) in a cold house?

We all know where motivation will be right then. It will be flushed down the toilet and have been replaced by rationalization. And rationalization is a crafty master—in seconds, we can convince ourselves that we need just a few extra minutes ...

... and the next thing we know, we're scrambling around the house late for work, late for life. Again.

It's a tricky problem. Just when we need our motivation the most—those first few moments of the day—is precisely when we seem to have the least of it.

The solution, then, is to boost that morning motivation and mount a surprise attack on rationalization. That's what the five steps that follow do. Each step in the process is designed to increase what Hal calls your Wake-Up Motivation Level (WUML).

First thing in the morning, you might have a low WUML, meaning you want nothing more than to go back to sleep when your alarm goes off. That's normal. But by using this process, you can reach a high WUML, where you're ready to jump up and embrace the day.

The Five-Minute Snooze-Proof Wake-Up Strategy

Minute One: Set Your Intentions Before Bed

The first key to waking up is to remember this: Your first thought in the morning is usually the last thought you had before you went to bed. I bet, for example, that you've had nights where you could hardly fall asleep because you were so excited about waking up the next morning. Whether it was Christmas morning or the start of a big vacation, as soon as the alarm clock sounded, you opened your eyes ready to jump out of bed and embrace the day. Why? It's because the last thought you had about the coming morning before you went to bed was positive.

On the other hand, if your last thought before bed was something like, *Oh gosh, I can't believe I have to get up in six hours—I'm going to be exhausted in the morning!* then your first thought when the alarm clock goes off is likely to be something like, *Oh my goodness, it's already been six hours? Nooo! I just want to keep sleeping!*

The first step, then, is to consciously decide every night to actively and mindfully create a positive expectation for the next morning. Just as it is so important to have a consistent bedtime routine for our children, we too can benefit from intentionally putting ourselves to sleep.

For help on this and to get the precise words to say before bed to create your powerful intentions, download *The Miracle Morning Bedtime Affirmations* free at www.TMMBook.com.

Minute Two: Walk *across the Room* to Turn off the Alarm

If you haven't already, move your alarm clock across the room. This forces you to get out of bed and engage your body in movement. Motion creates energy—getting all the way up and out of bed naturally helps you wake up.

If you keep your alarm clock next to your bed, you're still in a partial sleep state after the alarm goes off, and it makes it much more difficult to wake yourself up. In fact, you may turn off the alarm without even realizing it! On more than a few occasions, you might have convinced yourself that your alarm clock was merely part of the dream you were having. (You're not alone on that one, trust me.)

Simply forcing yourself to get out of bed to turn off the alarm clock will instantly increase your WUML. However, you'll likely still be feeling more sleepy than not. To raise that WUML just a little further, try ...

Minute Three: Brush Your Teeth

As soon as you've gotten out of bed and turned off your alarm clock, go directly to the bathroom sink to brush your teeth. While you're at it, splash some water on your face. This simple activity will increase your WUML even further.

Now that your mouth is fresh, it's time to ...

Minute Four: Drink a Full Glass of Water

It's crucial that you hydrate yourself first thing every morning. After six to eight hours without water, you'll be mildly dehydrated, which causes fatigue. Often when people feel tired—at any time of the day—what they really need is more water, not more sleep.

Start by getting a glass or bottle of water (or you can do what we do, and fill it up the night before so it's already there for you in the morning), and drink it as fast as is comfortable for you. The objective is to replace the water you were deprived of during the hours you slept. (And hey, the side benefits of morning hydration are better, younger-looking skin and maintaining a healthy weight. Not bad for a few ounces of water!)

That glass of water should raise your WUML another notch, which will get you to …

Minute Five: Get Dressed or Jump in the Shower

The fifth step has two options. Option one is to get dressed in your exercise clothes so you're ready to leave your bedroom and immediately engage in your *Miracle Morning*. You can either lay out your clothes before you go to bed or even sleep in your workout clothes. (Yes, really.) And for parents, the "night before" prep is especially important to help you go straight into your practice. You can make this part of your kids' bedtime ritual so they build the habit too.

Option two is to jump in the shower. I usually change into exercise clothes, since I'll need a shower after working out, but a lot of people prefer the morning shower because it helps them wake up and gives them a fresh start to the day. The choice is yours.

Regardless of which option you choose, by the time you've executed these five simple steps, your WUML should be high enough that it requires very little discipline to stay awake for your Miracle Morning.

If you were to try to make that commitment the moment your alarm clock first went off—while you were at a WUML of nearly zero—it would be a much more difficult decision to make. The five steps let you build momentum so that, within just a few minutes, you're ready to go instead of feeling groggy.

I have never made it through the first five minutes and decided to go back to bed. Once I am up and moving intentionally through the morning, it makes it much easier to continue being purposeful throughout the day.

Miracle Morning Bonus Wake-Up Tips

Although this strategy has worked for thousands of people, these five steps are not the only way to make waking up in the morning easier. Here are a few others I've heard from fellow Miracle Morning practitioners:

- *The Miracle Morning* "Bedtime Affirmations": If you haven't done this yet, take a moment now to go to www.TMMbook. com and download the re-energizing, intention-setting "Bedtime Affirmations" for free. Nothing is more effective for ensuring that you will wake up before your alarm than programming your mind to achieve exactly what you want.

- Set a timer for your bedroom lights: One of The Miracle Morning Community members sets his bedroom lights on a timer (you can buy an appliance timer online or at your local hardware store). As his alarm goes off, the lights come on in the room. What a great idea! It's a lot easier to fall back asleep when it's dark—having the lights on tells your mind and body that it's time to wake up. (Regardless of whether you use a timer, be sure to turn your light on first thing when your alarm goes off.)

- Set a timer for your bedroom heater: Another fan of *The Miracle Morning* says that in the winter, she keeps a bedroom heater on an appliance timer set to go off fifteen minutes before she wakes up. She keeps it cold at night, but warm for waking up so she won't be tempted to crawl back under her covers.

Feel free to add to or customize the Five-Minute Snooze-Proof Wake-Up Strategy, and if you have any tips that you're open to sharing, we'd love to hear them. Please post them in The Miracle Morning Community at www.MyTMMCommunity.com.

Waking up consistently and easily is all about having an effective, predetermined, step-by-step strategy to increase your WUML in the morning. Don't wait to try this! Start tonight by reading *The Miracle Morning* "Bedtime Affirmations," moving your alarm clock across the room, setting a glass of water on your nightstand, and committing to the other two steps for the morning.

How to Go from Unbearable to Unstoppable (in 30 Days)

Incorporating any new habit requires an adjustment period—don't expect this to be effortless from day one. But do make a commitment to yourself to stick with it. The seemingly unbearable first few days are only temporary. While there's a lot of debate about how long it takes to create a new habit, 30 days is definitely enough to test-drive your new morning routine.

As you take the Miracle Morning 30-Day Challenge, here's what you might expect as you build your new routine.

Phase One: Unbearable (Days 1–10)

Phase One is when any new activity requires tremendous effort, and getting up early is no different. You're fighting existing habits, the very habits that have been entrenched in *who you are* for years.

In this phase, it's mind over matter—and if you don't mind, it'll definitely matter! The habits of letting the kids wake you up, or hitting snooze if you have late-sleeping kids, and not making the most of your day are the same habits that hold you back from becoming the superstar parent you have always known you can be. So dig in and hold strong.

In Phase One, while you battle existing patterns and limiting beliefs, you'll find out what you're made of and what you're capable of. You need to keep pushing, stay committed to your vision, and hang in there. Trust me when I say you can do this!

I know it can be daunting on day five to realize you still have twenty-five days to go before your transformation is complete and you've become a bona fide morning person. Keep in mind that on day five, you're actually more than halfway through the first phase and well on your way. Remember: your initial feelings are not going to last forever. In fact, you owe it to yourself to persevere because, in no time at all, you'll be getting the exact results you want as you become the person you've always wanted to be!

Phase Two: Uncomfortable (Days 11–20)

In Phase Two, your body and mind begin to acclimate to waking up earlier. You'll notice that getting up starts to get a tiny bit easier, but it's not yet a habit—it's not quite who you are and likely won't feel natural yet.

The biggest temptation at this level is to reward yourself by taking a break, especially on the weekends. A question posted quite often in The Miracle Morning Community is, "How many days a week do you get up early for your Miracle Morning?" Our answer—and the one that's most common from longtime Miracle Morning practitioners— is *every single day*.

Once you've made it through Phase One, you're past the hardest period. So keep going! Why on earth would you want to go through that first phase again by taking one or two days off? Trust me, you wouldn't, so don't!

Phase Three: Unstoppable (Days 21–30)

Early rising is now not only a habit, it has literally become part of *who you are*, part of your identity. Your body and mind will have become accustomed to your new way of being. These next ten days are important for cementing the habit in yourself and your life.

As you engage in the Miracle Morning practice, you will also develop an appreciation for the three distinct phases of habit change. A side benefit is you will realize you can identify, develop, and adopt any habit that serves you—up to and including the habits of the exceptional parents we have included in this book.

What Do I DO with My Morning?

Thirty days, you might be thinking, *I can get up earlier for thirty days ... But what do I DO with that time?*

This is where the magic begins. I'm going to introduce you to the routines at the heart of the Miracle Morning. They're called the Life S.A.V.E.R.S., and they're the habits that are going to transform your mornings, yourself, and your family.

Taking Immediate Action

There's no need to wait to get started with creating your new, amazing future. As Anthony Robbins has said, "When is NOW a good time for you to do that?" Now, indeed, would be perfect! In fact, the sooner you start, the sooner you'll begin to see results, including increased energy, a better attitude, and, of course, a happier home life.

Step One: Set your alarm for one hour earlier than you usually wake up, and schedule that hour in your calendar to do your first Miracle Morning … tomorrow morning. If you've been letting your kids wake you up, stop. The key is to get up an hour before they do so that you can get your practice in before the onslaught!

From this day forward, starting with the next 30 days, keep your alarm set for 60 minutes earlier than your children typically wake up so that you can start waking up when you *want* to, instead of when you *have* to. It's time to start launching each day with a Miracle Morning so that you can become the person you need to be to take yourself, your children, and your family to extraordinary levels.

What will you do with that hour? You're going to find out in the next chapter, but for now, simply continue reading this book during your Miracle Morning until you learn the whole routine.

Step Two: Join The Miracle Morning Community at www.MyT-MMCommunity.com to connect with and get additional support from more than 40,000 like-minded early risers, many of whom have been generating extraordinary results with the Miracle Morning for years.

Step Three: Find a Miracle Morning accountability partner. Enroll someone—your spouse, a friend, family member, or coworker—to join you on this adventure and hold each other accountable to follow through until your Miracle Morning has become a lifelong habit.

— 3 —
THE LIFE S.A.V.E.R.S.
Six Practices Guaranteed To Save You From a Life of Unfulfilled Potential

What Hal has done with his acronym S.A.V.E.R.S. is take the best practices—developed over centuries of human consciousness development—and condensed the "best of the best" into a daily morning ritual. A ritual that is now part of my day.

Many people do one of the S.A.V.E.R.S. daily. For example, many people do the **E**, *they exercise every morning. Others do* **S** *for silence or meditation, or* **S** *for scribing or journaling. But until Hal packaged S.A.V.E.R.S., no one was doing all six ancient "best practices" every morning. The Miracle Morning is perfect for very busy, successful people. Going through S.A.V.E.R.S. every morning is like pumping rocket fuel into my body, mind, and spirit ... before I start my day, every day.*
—Robert Kiyosaki, Best-Selling author of *Rich Dad Poor Dad*

Having read the above quote, you may be thinking, *Well, that doesn't apply to me. I'm just a mom (or dad).* The phrase "very busy, successful people" is rarely used to describe parents. In fact, the word parent is more likely to conjure up images of a harried, overwhelmed person trying to survive each day. Whether the image includes a diaper bag or a folder of college applications, it's just as accurate. Being a parent today is a very demanding job.

And that's exactly why the Life S.A.V.E.R.S. were written especially for you.

When Hal experienced the second of his two rock bottoms, both of which you can read about in *The Miracle Morning*, he began his own quest for the fastest way to take his personal development to the next level. He went in search of the daily practices of the world's most successful people.

After discovering six of the most proven, timeless personal development practices, Hal first attempted to determine which one or two would accelerate his success the fastest. Then he asked, *What would happen if I did ALL of them?*

Why the Life S.A.V.E.R.S. Work

The Life S.A.V.E.R.S. are simple but profoundly effective daily morning practices that help you plan and live your life on your terms. They're designed to start your day in a peak physical, mental, emotional, and spiritual state so that you both continually improve and will ALWAYS perform at your best.

I know, I know. You don't have time. Before starting the Miracle Morning, we would wake up to pure chaos with barely enough time to get everyone dressed, fed, and out the door for the first activity of the day. I don't know how many times Tyler missed the school bus because I was not prepared, and as a kindergartener, he wasn't allowed to walk by himself. I often said, "Hurry up," and "Sorry you can't have eggs today. Mommy doesn't have time to make them for you." You probably think you can hardly squeeze in what you have to do already, never mind what you want to do. But I "didn't have time" before the Miracle Morning either. And yet, here I am with more time, more prosperity, and a more peaceful family than I've ever had.

What you need to realize right now is that your Miracle Morning will create time for you. The Life S.A.V.E.R.S. are the vehicle to help you reconnect with your true essence and wake up with purpose instead of obligation. The practices help you build energy, see priorities more clearly, and help you find the most productive flow in your life.

In other words, the Life S.A.V.E.R.S. don't take time from your day but ultimately add more to it.

Each letter in S.A.V.E.R.S. represents one of the best practices of the most successful people on the planet. And they're also the same activities that bring new levels of peace, clarity, motivation, and energy to your life. They are

Silence

Affirmations

Visualization

Exercise

Reading

Scribing

These practices are the best possible use of your newfound morning time. They're customizable to fit you, your life, and your goals. And you can start first thing tomorrow morning.

Let's go through each of the six practices in detail.

S is for Silence

Silence, the first practice of the Life S.A.V.E.R.S., is a key habit for parents. If you're surrounded by the endless barrage of hungry kids, homework assignments, art projects that have expanded onto the walls, a knee-deep layer of toys on the floor in every room, meal planning, diapers, or dirty clothes, then this is your opportunity to STOP and BREATHE!

Like we did before the Miracle Morning, most people start the day when their kids bounce into the room, raring to go. And most people run from morning to night, struggling to regain control for the rest of the day. It's not a coincidence. Starting each day with a period of silence instead will immediately reduce your stress levels and help you begin the day with the kind of calm and clarity that you need to focus on what's most important.

For parents, who are surrounded with energetic children, silence is perhaps the rarest commodity. Remember, many of the world's most successful people are daily practitioners of silence. That shows you how important it is. It's not surprising that Oprah practices stillness—or that she does nearly all the other Life S.A.V.E.R.S. too. Musician Katy Perry practices transcendental meditation as do Sheryl Crow and Sir Paul McCartney. Film and television stars Jennifer Aniston, Ellen DeGeneres, Jerry Seinfeld, Howard Stern, Cameron Diaz, Clint Eastwood, and Hugh Jackman have all spoken of their daily meditation practice. Hip-hop mogul Russell Simmons meditates with his two daughters every morning for 20 minutes. Even famous billionaires Ray Dalio and Rupert Murdoch have attributed their financial success to the daily practice of stillness. You'll be in good (and quiet) company by doing the same.

If it seems like I'm asking you to do nothing, let me clarify: you have a number of choices for your practice of silence. In no particular order, here are a few to get you started:

- Meditation
- Prayer
- Reflection
- Deep breathing
- Gratitude

Whichever you choose, be sure you don't stay in bed for your period of silence, and better still, get out of your bedroom altogether.

In an interview with *Shape Magazine*, actress and singer Kristen Bell said, "Do meditative yoga for 10 minutes every morning. When you have a problem—whether it's road rage, your guy, or work—meditation allows everything to unfold the way it's supposed to."

And don't be afraid to expand your horizons. Meditation comes in many forms. As Angelina Jolie told *Stylist Magazine*, "I find meditation in sitting on the floor with the kids coloring for an hour, or going on the trampoline. You do what you love, that makes you happy, and that gives you your meditation."

The Benefits of Silence

How many times as parents do we find ourselves in stressful situations? How many times do we deal with immediate needs that take us away from our vision or plan? Stress is one of the most common side effects of parenting. We face the ever-present distractions of other people encroaching on our schedule and the inevitable fires we must extinguish. Our kids have the uncanny ability to push our stress buttons. They let us know they have to pee as we get on the highway (after we'd asked them five minutes prior if they had to go). They draw on freshly painted walls with permanent markers. Or maybe they throw an iPad in anger and break the screen.

Excessive stress is terrible for your health. It triggers your fight-or-flight response, and that releases a cascade of toxic hormones that can stay in your body for days. That's fine if you experience that type of stress only occasionally. But when the constant assault of life with children keeps the adrenaline flowing all the time, the negative impact on your health adds up. Quieting the mind allows you to put those things aside and focus on you and your parenting vision.

Silence in the form of meditation reduces stress, and as a result, improves your health. A major study run by several groups, including the National Institutes of Health, the American Medical Association, the Mayo Clinic, and scientists from both Harvard and Stanford, revealed that meditation reduces stress and high blood pressure. A recent study by Dr. Norman Rosenthal, a world-renowned psychiatrist who works with the David Lynch Foundation, even found that people who practice meditation are 30 percent less likely to die from heart disease.

Another study from Harvard found that just eight weeks of meditation could lead to "increased gray-matter density in the hippocampus, known to be important for learning and memory, and in structures associated with self-awareness, compassion, and introspection."

Meditation helps you to slow down and focus on you, even if it's for just a short time. Start your meditation practice and say goodbye to "mommy brain."

"I started meditating because I felt like I needed stop my life from running me," singer Sheryl Crow has said. "So meditation for me helped slow my day down." She continues to devote 20 minutes in the morning and 20 minutes at night to meditation.

Monica Dix, a mom in the Miracle Morning Community shared this story. At breakfast, her five-year-old daughter told her, "I like when you pretend you're on top of a mountain." Monica asked her what she meant, and she responded, "When you're pretending that you're on a mountain and the sky is clear and you're just breathing." Monica asked, "Do you mean when I am meditating?" and her daughter replied, "Yes!" She paused then added, "I wish you would do it more, you're being a good mama." It's so encouraging when our children see the effort we are putting in for their benefit and cheer us on!

When you are silent, it opens a space for you to secure your own oxygen mask, before assisting others. The benefits are extraordinary and can bring you much needed clarity and peace of mind. Practicing silence, in other words, can help you reduce your stress, improve cognitive performance, and become a confident parent at the same time.

Guided Meditations and Meditation Apps

Meditation is like anything else—if you've never done it before, then it can be difficult or feel awkward at first. If you are a first time meditator, I recommend starting with a guided meditation.

Here are a few of my favorite meditation apps that are available for both iPhone/iPad and Android devices:

- Headspace
- Calm
- Omvana
- Simply Being
- Insight Timer

There are subtle and significant differences among these meditation apps, one of which is the voice of the person speaking.

If you don't have a device that allows you to download apps, simply go to YouTube or Google and search for the keywords "Guided Meditation." Our Spirit Coach® Jenai Lane has a free five-minute guided meditation available on her website, which you can access here: http://www.spiritcoachtraining.com/5min/. This is how Mike and I started our meditation practice.

Miracle Morning (Individual) Meditation

When you're ready to try meditating on your own, here is a simple, step-by-step meditation you can use during your Miracle Morning, even if you've never done this before.

- Before beginning, it's important to prepare yourself and set expectations. This is a time for you to quiet your mind and let go of the compulsive need to constantly be thinking about something—reliving the past or worrying about the future, but never living fully in the present. This is the time to let go of your stresses, take a break from worrying about your problems, and be here in this moment. It is a time to access the essence of who you truly are—to go deeper than what you have, what you do, or the labels you've accepted as who you are. If this sounds foreign to you, or too new agey, that's okay. I've felt the same way. It's probably because you've never tried it before. But thankfully, you're about to.

- Find a quiet, comfortable place to sit. You can sit on the couch, on a chair, on the floor, or on a pillow for added comfort.

- Sit upright, cross-legged. You can close your eyes, or you can look down at a point on the ground about two feet in front of you.

- Begin by focusing on your breath, taking slow, deep breaths. Breathe in through the nose and out through the mouth. The most effective breathing causes your belly to expand and not your chest.

- Now start pacing your breath; breathe in slowly for a count of three seconds (one one thousand, two one thousand, three one thousand), hold it in for another three counts, and then breathe out slowly for a final count of three. Feel your thoughts and emotions settling down as you focus on your breath. Be aware that, as you attempt to quiet your mind, thoughts will still come in to pay a visit. Simply acknowledge them and then let them go, always returning your focus to your breath.

- Allow yourself to be fully present in this moment. This is often referred to as being. Not thinking, not doing, just being. Continue to follow your breath, and imagine inhaling positive, loving, and peaceful energy and exhaling all your worries and stress. Enjoy the quiet. Enjoy the moment. Just breathe … Just be.

- If you find that you have a constant influx of thoughts, it may be helpful for you to focus on a single word, phrase, or mantra and repeat it over and over again to yourself as you inhale and exhale. For example, you might try something like this: (On the inhale) "I inhale confidence …" (As you exhale) "I exhale fear …" You can swap the word confidence for whatever you feel you need to bring more of into your life (love, faith, energy, etc.), and swap the word fear with whatever you feel you need to let go of (stress, worry, resentment, etc.).

Meditation is a gift you can give yourself every day. My time spent meditating has become one of my favorite parts of the Miracle Morning routine. It's a time to be at peace and to experience gratitude and freedom from my day-to-day stressors and worries.

Think of daily meditation as a temporary vacation from your problems. Although your problems will still be there when you finish your daily meditation, you'll find that you're more centered and better equipped to solve them.

A is for Affirmations

Have you ever wondered why some of the best parents around you seem to be on top of everything? Or why others seem to drop every ball? Time and time again, I suspect it is a parent's *mindset* that shows up as the driving factor in their effectiveness.

Teachers, other parents, doctors, and especially your children can sense your mindset. It shows up undeniably in your language, your confidence, and your demeanor. Your attitude affects the entire parenting process, whether you're feeding your child breakfast in the morning or picking them up from detention. Show me someone with a great mindset, and I'll show you a great parent.

I know firsthand, though, how difficult it can be to maintain confidence and enthusiasm—not to mention motivation—during the roller coaster ride that begins the day you bring your baby home from the hospital. Mindset is largely something we adopt without conscious thought—at a subconscious level, we have been programmed to think, believe, act, and talk to ourselves a certain way.

Our programming comes from many influences, including what others have told us, what we tell ourselves, and all of our good and bad life experiences. That programming expresses itself in every area of our lives, including the way we behave around our children. And that means, if we want a better family dynamic, we need better mental programming.

Affirmations are a tool for doing just that. They enable you to become more intentional about your goals while also providing the encouragement and positive mindset necessary to achieve them. When you repeatedly tell yourself who you want to be, what you want to accomplish, and how you are going to achieve it, your subconscious mind will shift your beliefs and behavior. Once you believe and act in new ways, you will begin to manifest your affirmations into reality.

Science has proven that affirmations—when done correctly—are one of the most effective tools for quickly becoming the person you need to be to achieve everything you want in your life—for yourself and your children. And yet, affirmations also get a bad rap. Many people have tried them only to be disappointed with little or no results.

Why the Old Way of Doing Affirmations Doesn't Work

For decades, countless so-called experts and gurus have taught affirmations in ways that have proven to be ineffective and set people up for failure. Here are two of the most common problems with affirmations.

Lying to Yourself Doesn't Work

I am the best parent in the world. No, you're not.

I have 7 percent body fat. No, you don't.

I have achieved all of my goals this year. Nope. Sorry, you haven't.

Creating affirmations as if you've already become or achieved something may be the single biggest reason that affirmations haven't worked for most people.

With this technique, every time you recite the affirmation that isn't rooted in truth, your subconscious will resist it. As an intelligent human being who isn't delusional, lying to yourself repeatedly will never be the optimum strategy. *The truth will always prevail.*

Passive Language Doesn't Produce Results

Many affirmations have been designed to make you feel good by creating an empty promise of something you desire. For example, here is a popular money affirmation that's been perpetuated by many world-famous gurus:

I am a money magnet. Money flows to me effortlessly and in abundance.

This type of affirmation might make you feel good in the moment by giving you a false sense of relief from your financial worries, but it won't generate any income. People who sit back and wait for money to show up magically are cash poor.

To generate the kind of abundance you want (or any result you desire, for that matter), you've got to actually do something. Your actions must be in alignment with your desired results, and your affirmations must articulate and affirm both.

Four Steps to Create Affirmations That Improve Your Parenting Skills

Here are simple steps to create and implement results-oriented Miracle Morning affirmations that will program your conscious and subconscious mind to produce results and take your levels of personal and parenting success beyond what you've ever experienced before.

Step One: The Extraordinary Result You Are Committed to and Why

Notice I'm not starting with what you want. Everyone wants things, but we don't get what we want: we get what we're committed to. You want to be a great role model for your kids? Who doesn't? Join that nonexclusive club. Oh wait, you're 100 percent committed to becoming a great role model for your kids by clarifying and executing the necessary actions until the result is achieved? Okay, now we're talking.

Action: Start by writing down a specific, extraordinary result or outcome—one that challenges you and would significantly improve your family life and one that you are ready to commit to creating even if you're not yet sure how you will do it. Then reinforce your commitment by including your *why*, the compelling reason you're willing to commit.

Examples: *I am dedicated to going on a date night once a week with my significant other to model a healthy love relationship for my children.*

Or ...

I am 100 percent committed to being as healthy as I can be so that I have the energy to be fully present with my children and spouse. Or ...

I am committed to doubling my income in the next 12 months, from $_____ to $_____, so that I can provide financial security for my family.

Step Two: The Necessary Actions You Are Committed to Taking and When

Writing an affirmation that merely affirms what you *want* without affirming what you are committed to *doing* is one step above pointless and can actually be counterproductive by tricking your subconscious mind into thinking that the result will happen automatically, without effort.

Action: Clarify the (specific) action, activity, or habit that is required for you to achieve your ideal outcome, and clearly state when and how often you will execute the necessary action.

Examples: *To ensure I have a date night weekly with my significant other, I am 100 percent committed to lining up a babysitter and choosing an activity by Wednesday of each week for the upcoming weekend and blocking that time on my calendar.*

Or ...

To ensure that I am as healthy as I can be, I am 100 percent committed to going to the gym five days per week and running on the treadmill for a minimum of 20 minutes each day from 6:00 a.m. to 7:00 a.m.

Or …

To guarantee that I double my income, I am committed to doubling my daily prospecting calls from 20 to 40 calls five days a week from 8:00 a.m. to 9:00 a.m.—NO MATTER WHAT.

The more specific your actions are, the better. Be sure to include *frequency* (how often), *quantity* (how many), and *precise time frames* (when you will begin and end your activities).

Step Three: Recite Your Affirmations Every Morning with Emotion

Remember, your Miracle Morning affirmations aren't designed merely to make you *feel good*. These written statements are strategically engineered to program your subconscious mind with the beliefs and mindset you need to achieve your desired outcomes while directing your conscious mind to keep you focused on your highest priorities and taking the actions that will get you there.

For your affirmations to be effective, however, it is important that you tap into your emotions while reciting them. Mindlessly repeating an affirmation without intentionally feeling its truth will have minimal impact for you. You must take responsibility for generating authentic emotions, such as excitement and determination, and powerfully infuse those emotions in every affirmation you recite.

You must affirm who you need to be to do the things you need to do so that you can have the results that you want. I'll say this again: It isn't magic; this strategy works when you connect with *the person you need to become* on the way to achieving your goals. It's who you are that attracts your results more than any other activity.

Action: Schedule time each day to read your affirmations during your Miracle Morning to both program your subconscious and focus your conscious mind on what's most important to you and what you are committed to doing to make it your reality. That's right, you must read them daily. Reading your affirmation occasionally is as effective as an occasional workout. You'll start seeing results only when you've made them a part of your daily routine.

A great place to read affirmations is in the shower. If you laminate them and leave them there, then they will be in front of you every day. Put them anywhere you can to remind you: under your car's sun visor, taped to your mirror. The more you see them, the more the subconscious mind can connect with them to change your thinking and your actions. You can even write them directly on a mirror with dry erase markers.

Step Four: Constantly Update and Evolve Your Affirmations

As you continue to grow, improve, and evolve, so should your affirmations. When you come up with a new goal, dream, or any extraordinary result you want to create for your life, add it to your affirmations.

Personally, I have affirmations for every single significant area of my life (finances, health, happiness, relationships, parenting, etc.), and I continually update them as I learn more. And I am always on the lookout for quotes, strategies, and philosophies that I can add to improve my mindset. Any time you come across an empowering quote or philosophy and think to yourself, *Wow, that is an area where I could make a huge improvement*, add it to your affirmations.

Remember, your affirmations should be tailored to you. Mike and I each have our own unique set because these are things we are *personally* committed to. They must be specific for them to work in your subconscious. As soon as you put the word "we" into an affirmation, it gives your mind permission to blame someone else if it does not come to fruition.

Your programming can change and improve at any time, starting right now. You can reprogram any perceived limitations with new beliefs and create new behaviors so you can become as successful as you want to be in any area of life you choose.

In summary, your new affirmations articulate the extraordinary results you are committed to creating, why they are critically important to you, and, most importantly, which necessary actions you are committed to taking and when to ensure that you attain and sustain the extraordinary levels of success you truly want (and deserve) for your life.

Affirmations to Become an Exceptional Parent

In addition to the formula to create your affirmations, I have included this list of sample affirmations, which may help spark your creativity. Feel free to include any of these that resonate with you.

- I am fully committed to protecting 30 minutes of my time daily for each of my children so they know they are important to me.

- I am fully committed to providing five healthy dinners a week for my family because I know my kids will pick up my eating habits, and I want them to have the healthiest start in life.

- I am absolutely committed to waking up at _____ every morning with the intention of getting my Miracle Morning in before the kids wake up so I can fill my cup in order to serve them when they wake.

- I focus on learning new things and improving my parenting skills daily, and I commit to reading or rereading at least one new book to help that effort every month.

- I continue to get to know my children by spending time with them and truly listening to them and their friends so that I will know when I need to take action and what type of action is necessary.

- I am committed to constant and never-ending improvement in the tasks necessary for the day-to-day functioning of my family.

- I commit to an unplugged family meal five nights a week so that we can strengthen our family as a group and stay connected to each other.

- I am committed to empowering my children with the knowledge and skills that I learn so that they can self-sufficiently attain any level of success that they wish in life.

- I am committed to learning from my children and being open to the lessons they have to teach me, including their visions of what they want to be not what I want them to be.

- I am committed to reading for 20 minutes with each of my children every day.

These are just a few examples of affirmations. You can use any that resonate with you, but do create your own using the four-step formula described in the previous pages. Anything you repeat to yourself over and over again with emotion will be programmed into your subconscious mind, help you form new beliefs, and manifest through your actions.

V is for Visualization

Visualization is a technique for using your imagination to create what you want in life.

Top athletes use visualization to enhance their performance. Olympic athletes and top performers in many categories incorporate this process as a critical part of their daily training. What is less well known is that confident parents, the truly exceptional ones, use it just as frequently.

If you'd like some fascinating information about *why* visualization works, just Google mirror neurons. A neuron is a cell that connects the brain and other parts of the body; a mirror neuron fires when we take an action or observe someone else taking an action. This is a relatively new area of study in neurology, but these cells seem to allow us to improve our abilities by watching other people perform them *or* by visualizing ourselves performing them. Some studies indicate that experienced weight lifters can increase muscle mass through vivid visualization sessions, and mirror neurons get the credit for making this possible. In many ways, the brain can't tell the difference between a vivid visualization and an actual experience. Crazy, right?

I was always a little skeptical about the value of visualization because it sounded a little too new agey. Once I read about mirror neurons, my whole attitude changed!

What Do You Visualize?

Most parents are limited by visions of their past results, replaying previous failures and heartbreaks. Creative visualization, on the other hand, enables you to design the vision that will occupy your mind, ensuring that the greatest pull on you is your future—a compelling, exciting, and limitless future.

After I've read my affirmations, I sit upright, close my eyes, and take a few slow, deep breaths. For the next five to ten minutes, I simply visualize the *specific actions* that are necessary for my long- and short-term goals to become a reality.

Notice that I did *not* say that I visualize the results. Many people will disagree on this, but some studies show that visualizing the victory (for example, standing on stage, the new car, the dream house, the new team member, etc.) can actually diminish your drive because your brain has already experienced the reward on some level. Instead, I recommend using visualization as a practice session for improving the skills or aspects of your life you are working on. Visualize actions not results. Imagine yourself putting in the work, like Rocky running through the streets of Philadelphia and chasing hens around with Mickey motivating him in the background. Don't simply imagine him delivering the knockout blow and being crowned the champion; get in touch with the effort required to get him here. Get comfortable being uncomfortable by practicing, embracing, and choosing to experience the actions necessary for success.

You might picture yourself having fun and light conversations with your children. Spend time imagining your family talking at dinner, for example. What does it look like? How does it feel as you develop a great relationship? Picture yourself responding to obstacles and issues.

If bedtime is a chore for your family like it used to be for us, you can visualize yourself calmly supporting the kids as they get ready for bed. Imagine yourself lovingly helping them brush their teeth and see them excitedly choosing a bedtime story. Imagine yourself reading the story with enthusiasm, asking questions about what you are reading, and truly enjoying the time you get to spend with them before they drift off to sleep. Imagine how peaceful they are as they sleep and giving them a final goodnight kiss on the forehead.

You can pick anything that is a critical action step or skill that you may not be performing at your best yet. Envisioning success and what it takes to get there will prepare you for, and almost ensure, a successful day.

Three Simple Steps for Miracle Morning Visualization

The perfect time to visualize yourself living in alignment with your affirmations is right after you read them.

Step One: Get Ready

Some people like to play instrumental music in the background during their visualization, such as classical or baroque (check out anything from the composer J. S. Bach). If you'd like to experiment with music, put it on with the volume relatively low. Personally, I find anything with words to be a distraction.

Now, sit up tall in a comfortable position. This can be on a chair, the couch, or the floor with a cushion. Breathe deeply. Close your eyes, clear your mind, and get ready to visualize.

Step Two: Visualize What You Really Want

The greatest gift you can give to the people you love is to live up to your full potential. What does that look like for you? What do you really want? Forget about logic, limits, and being practical. If you could have, do, or be anything you wanted, what would you choose? What *specific actions* would you have to take to achieve it? Who would you have to become? How would you act in different situations?

See, feel, hear, touch, taste, and smell every detail of your vision. Involve all your senses to maximize effectiveness. The more vivid you make your vision, the more compelled you'll be to take the necessary actions to make it a reality.

Step Three: Visualize Who You Need to Be and What You Need to Do

Once you've created a clear mental picture of what you want, begin to visualize yourself living in total alignment with the person you need to be to achieve your vision. See yourself engaged in the positive actions you'll need to do each day (exercising, studying, working, spending time with your kids, family interactions, etc.), and make sure you see yourself enjoying the process. See yourself smiling as you're running on that trail listening to the lovely sound of birds singing, feeling the cool shade on your back, and feeling a sense of pride for your self-discipline to follow through.

Picture the look of determination on your face as you confidently and consistently connect with your children, listen to their needs, and take action based on what you observe. Visualize your family, friends, and spouse responding to your positive demeanor and optimistic outlook.

See yourself as the parent who has it all together. You arrive five minutes early to everything, and you're fully prepared (with extras even!). Imagine yourself joyfully sitting down with your planner and organizing the upcoming days and weeks with playdates, mom's nights, self-care appointments, date nights, and school activities. Visualize yourself writing thank-you notes by hand to your children's teachers as your young ones sit next to you writing their own. Imagine the kids helping to chop the vegetables you've grown in your organic backyard garden, and smell the delicious, healthy dinner cooking. Picture the whole family sitting around the dinner table laughing and smiling as you all thoroughly enjoy each bite.

Final Thoughts on Visualization

When you combine reading your affirmations every morning with daily visualization, you will turbocharge the programming of your subconscious mind for success. When you include this practice, you begin to align your thoughts and feelings with your vision to make it your reality. You can more easily maintain the motivation to continue taking the necessary actions. Visualization is a powerful aid in overcoming self-limiting habits, such as procrastination, to do what needs to be done to achieve your goals.

E is for Exercise

Exercise should be a staple of your Miracle Morning. Even a few minutes of exercise each day significantly enhances your health, improves your self-confidence and emotional well-being, and enables you to think better and concentrate longer. You'll also notice how quickly your energy increases with daily exercise, and your family will notice it too.

Personal development experts and self-made multimillionaire entrepreneurs Eben Pagan and Tony Robbins (who is also a bestselling author) both agree that the number one key to success is to start every morning with a personal success ritual. Included in both of their success rituals is some type of morning exercise. If it's good enough for Eben and Tony, it's good enough for me!

Lest you think you have to engage in triathlon or marathon training, think again. Your morning exercise also doesn't need to replace an afternoon or evening regimen if you already have one in place. You can still hit the gym at the usual time. However, the benefits from adding as little as five minutes of morning exercise are undeniable, including improved blood pressure and blood sugar levels and decreased risk of all kinds of scary things like heart disease, osteoporosis, cancer, and diabetes. Maybe most importantly, a little exercise in the morning will increase your energy levels for the rest of the day to help you keep up with your energetic offspring.

You can go for a walk or run, follow along to a yoga video on YouTube, or find a Life S.A.V.E.R.S. buddy and play some early morning racquetball. There's also an excellent app called 7 Minute Workout that gives you a full body workout in—you guessed it—seven minutes. The choice is yours, but pick one activity and do it.

As a parent, you are constantly on the go. You need an endless reserve of energy to make the best of the challenges that come your way, and a daily morning exercise practice is going to provide it.

Exercise for Your Brain

Even if you don't care about your physical health, consider that exercise is simply going to make you smarter, and that can only help your problem-solving abilities. Dr. Steven Masley, a Florida physician and nutritionist with a health practice geared toward executives, explains how exercise creates a direct connection to your cognitive ability.

"If we're talking about brain performance, the best predictor of brain speed is aerobic capacity—how well you can run up a hill is very strongly correlated with brain speed and cognitive shifting ability," Masley said.

Masley has designed a corporate wellness program based on the work he's done with more than 1,000 patients. "The average person going into these programs will increase brain speed by 25–30 percent."

Imagine how a 25–30 percent increase in brain speed could increase your ability to respond to your children in a positive way and offer helpful solutions. How much could you improve your parenting by having more effective and efficient conversations with your partner and children? For example, picture yourself settling a fight between your children after a workout. What would your state of mind be? How different would you feel? What would the kids gain from these conversations? What might that do for your family?

Hal chose yoga for his exercise activity and began practicing it shortly after he created the Miracle Morning. He's been doing it and loving it ever since. Our exercise routines differ. Mike typically does some yoga poses and practices tae kwon do as part of his Miracle Morning and then goes for a run close to home or hits the gym for some weights or yoga class. I head to the gym (where they have childcare) every weekday and attend a group fitness class or go for a run while listening to audiobooks. We keep a mini trampoline in our meditation room and often say our affirmations while bouncing. On the weekends, we like to run together or do something active as a family. We enjoy the variety. Find what resonates with you and make it a part of your Miracle Morning.

Final Thoughts on Exercise

You know that if you want to maintain good health and increase your energy, you must exercise consistently. That's not news to anyone. But what also isn't news is how easy it is to make excuses. Two of the biggest are "I don't have time" and "I'm too tired." And those are just the first two on the list. There is no limit to the excuses you can think of. And the more creative you are, the more excuses you can find!

That's the beauty of incorporating exercise into your Miracle Morning—it happens before your day wears you out and before you have an entire day to come up with new excuses. Because it comes first, the Miracle Morning is a surefire way to avoid those excuses and make exercise a daily habit.

Legal disclaimer: Hopefully this goes without saying, but you should consult your doctor or physician before beginning any exercise regimen, especially if you are experiencing any physical pain, discomfort, disabilities, etc. You may need to modify or even refrain from an exercise routine to meet your individual needs.

R is for Reading

Not only are you a role model for your children, but one of the fastest ways to achieve everything you want is to find successful people to be your role models. For every goal you have, there's a good chance an expert out there has already achieved the same thing or something similar. As Tony Robbins says, "Success leaves clues."

Fortunately, some of the best of the best have shared their stories in writing. And that means all those success blueprints are just waiting for anyone willing to invest the time in reading. Books are a limitless supply of help and mentorship right at your fingertips.

Occasionally, I hear somebody say, "I'm just not a big reader." I get it. I never considered myself a big reader either. In school I had to attend special reading classes, and on standardized tests, I always received low marks for reading comprehension. I feared reading aloud to my kids and showing them that Mommy isn't a great reader and messed up the book.

I had that attitude until I read Paul Kropp's book *How to Make Your Child a Reader for Life*. He writes, "As a parent, you are essential in making sure that books and the sheer joy of reading are part of your child's experience. No one can encourage reading nearly as well as you can. No other skill you teach or gift you give will ever be quite as important." The best way to create a reader for life in your child is to become one yourself! Since you are reading this book, you are probably aware of this and have already taken the steps to enjoy the benefits of reading. After I learned these facts about reading aloud to my kids and the importance of reading for lifelong learning, I committed to reading 24 books in a year, and it changed my outlook.

Here are some of our favorites that will specifically help you improve your parenting and family relationships. This is just a sample of the great books available for all types of parents with kids of all ages. One caveat: not every parenting book will work for every family. Pay close attention to whether a book is taking you in a direction that feels right to you. Trust your instincts as a parent first.

On Parenting:

- *The Available Parent: Radical Optimism for Raising Teens and Tweens* by Dr. John Duffy

- *The Conscious Parent: Transforming Ourselves, Empowering Our Children* by Dr. Shefali Tsabary

- *Sitting Still Like a Frog: Mindfulness Exercises for Kids (and Their Parents)* by Eline Snel and Myla Kabat-Zinn

- *The Opposite of Spoiled: Raising Kids Who Are Grounded, Generous, and Smart About Money* by Ron Lieber

- *The Family Board Meeting* by Jim Sheils

- *Yell Less, Love More: How the Orange Rhino Mom Stopped Yelling at Her Kids—and How You Can Too!* by Sheila McCraith

- *The 5 Love Languages of Children* by Gary D. Chapman and Ross Campbell

- *The Whole-Brain Child: 12 Revolutionary Strategies to Nurture Your Child's Developing Mind* by Daniel J. Siegel and Tina Payne Bryson

- *Scientific Secrets for Raising Kids Who Thrive* by The Great Courses and Professor Peter M. Vishton

- *Guerrilla Learning: How to Give Your Kids a Real Education with or without School* by Grace Llewellyn

- *Your Child's Strengths: A Guide for Parents and Teachers* by Jenifer Fox

- *The Successful Single Mom: Get Your Life Back and Your Game On!* by Honorée Corder

- *The Gift of Failure: How the Best Parents Learn to Let Go So Their Children Can Succeed* by Jessica Lahey

- *Peaceful Parent, Happy Kids: How to Stop Yelling and Start Connecting* by Dr. Laura Markham

On Mindset:

- *The Art of Exceptional Living* by Jim Rohn
- *The One Thing: The Surprisingly Simple Truth Behind Extraordinary Results* by Gary Keller and Jay Papasan
- *The 7 Habits of Highly Effective People: Powerful Lessons in Personal Change* by Stephen R. Covey
- *Mastery* by Robert Greene
- *The 4 Hour Workweek: Escape 9-5, Live Anywhere, and Join the New Rich* by Tim Ferriss
- *The Game of Life and How to Play It* by Florence Scovel Shinn
- *The Compound Effect* by Darren Hardy
- *Taking Life Head On: How to Love the Life You Have While You Create the Life of Your Dreams* by Hal Elrod
- *Think and Grow Rich* by Napoleon Hill
- *Vision to Reality: How Short Term Massive Action Equals Long Term Maximum Results* by Honorée Corder
- *Finding Your Element: How to Discover Your Talents and Passions and Transform Your Life* by Sir Ken Robinson and Lou Aronica
- *Spirit Led Instead: The Little Tool Book of Limitless Transformation* by Jenai Lane

In addition to finding parenting confidence, you can transform your relationships, increase your self-confidence, improve your communication skills, learn how to become healthy, and improve any other area of your life you can think of. Head to your library or local bookstore—or do what we do and visit Amazon.com—and you'll find more books than you can possibly imagine on any area of your life you want to improve.

For a complete list of Hal's favorite personal development books—including those that have made the biggest impact on his success and happiness—check out the Recommended Reading list at TMMBook.com.

How Much Should You Read?

I recommend making a commitment to read a minimum of ten pages per day (although five is okay to start with if you read slowly or don't yet enjoy reading).

Ten pages does not seem like much, but let's do the math. Reading ten pages a day gives you 3,650 pages a year. That stacks up to approximately eighteen 200-page personal development or self-improvement books! All in 10–15 minutes of reading, or 15–30 minutes if you read more slowly.

If you read 18 personal development or parenting books in the next year, do you think you'll be more knowledgeable, capable, and confident? Do you think you'll be a better you? Absolutely! Reading 10 pages per day is not going to break you, but it will surely make you.

Final Thoughts on Reading

- Begin with the end in mind—what do you hope to gain from the book? Take a moment to do this now by asking yourself what you want to gain from reading this one.

- Books don't have to be read cover to cover, nor do they have to be finished. Remember that this is *your* reading time. Use the table of contents to make sure you are reading the parts you care about most, and don't hesitate to put it down and move to another book if you aren't enjoying it. There is too much incredible information out there to spend any time on the mediocre.

- Many Miracle Morning practitioners use their reading time to catch up on their religious texts, such as the Bible or Torah.

- Unless you're borrowing a book from the library or a friend, feel free to underline, circle, highlight, dog-ear, and take notes in the margins of the book. The process of marking books as you read allows you to come back at any time and recapture the key lessons, ideas, and benefits without needing to read the book again cover to cover. If you read on a digital reader, such as Kindle, Nook, or via iBooks, notes and highlighting are easily organized, so you can see them each time you flip through the book, or you can go directly to a list of your notes and highlights.

- Summarize key ideas, insights, and memorable passages in a journal. You can build your own summary of your favorite books so you can revisit the key content any time in just minutes.

- Rereading good personal development books is an underused yet very effective strategy. Rarely can you read a book once and internalize all of its value. Achieving mastery in any area requires repetition. I've read *Spirit Lead Instead* by Jenai Lane as many as three times and often refer back to it throughout the year. Why not try it out with this book? Commit to re-reading it as soon as you're finished to deepen your learning and give yourself more time to master your Miracle Morning.

- Audiobooks count as reading! You still get the information, and you can do it while exercising or during your commute. When I really want to study a book, I listen to the audio while looking at the text. This way I can take notes and underline text without slowing down too much. I am a pretty slow reader, but with audiobooks, I can listen at 1.5X or 2X speed and read much faster.

- Take advantage of action steps and action plans set out in the books you read. While reading is a great way to learn new strategies, it is the internalization and practice of new strategies that will improve your life. Are you committed to implementing what you're learning in this book by taking action and following through with a 30-Day Challenge at the end?

S is for Scribing

Scribing is simply another word for writing. I write in my journal for ten to fifteen minutes during my Miracle Morning, usually during reading time, and then during an additional period when I focus on gratitude. By getting your thoughts out of your head and putting them on the page, you gain valuable insights you'd otherwise never see.

The scribing element of your Miracle Morning enables you to document your visions, insights, ideas, breakthroughs, realizations, successes, and lessons learned as well as any areas of opportunity, personal growth, or improvement. Use your journal to note your parenting strengths and successes, what went right each day, and any insights you want to remember later and perhaps work on.

If you're like Hal used to be, you probably have at least a few half-used and barely touched journals and notebooks. It wasn't until he started his own Miracle Morning practice that scribing quickly became a favored habit. As Tony Robbins has said many times, "A life worth living is a life worth recording."

Writing will give you the daily benefits of consciously directing your thoughts, but what's even more powerful are the insights you'll gain from reviewing your journals, from cover to cover, afterwards especially at the end of the year.

It is hard to put into words how overwhelmingly constructive the experience of going back and reviewing your journals can be. Michael Maher, *The Miracle Morning for Real Estate Agents* coauthor, is an avid practitioner of the Life S.A.V.E.R.S. Part of Michael's morning routine is to write down his appreciations and affirmations in what he calls his Blessings Book. Michael says it best:

"What you appreciate ... APPRECIATES. It is time to take our insatiable appetite for what we want and replace it with an insatiable appetite and gratitude for what we do have. Write your appreciations, be grateful and appreciative, and you will have more of those things you crave—better relationships, more material goods, more happiness."

There is strength in writing down what you appreciate, and reviewing this material can change your mindset on a challenging day. A great practice to add to your routine is to write what you appreciate about each of your children, your significant other, and especially yourself. When we write down the things we appreciate about our kids and spouse, even (and particularly) when they are not on their best behavior, it's easier to focus on their positive qualities.

For example, you may be angry with your son because he hit your daughter, but afterwards he attempted to comfort her. Instead of focusing on his poor choice, be grateful for his compassion after the fact. Another example would be when your spouse is late for your date night. It would be easy to get angry, but instead you can feel grateful that he arrived safely and that you're out of the house and away from the kids!

While there are many worthwhile benefits of keeping a daily journal, here are a few more of my favorites. With daily scribing, you'll

- Gain Clarity—Journaling will give you more clarity and understanding and allow you to brainstorm as well as help you work through problems.

- Capture Ideas—You will capture and be able to expand on your ideas, and journaling also prevents you from losing the important ones you are saving for an opportune moment in the future.

- Review Lessons—Journaling provides a place to reference and review all of the lessons you've learned.

- Acknowledge Your Progress—It's wonderful to go back and read your journal entries from a year ago to see how much progress you've made. It's one of the most empowering, confidence-inspiring, and enjoyable experiences. It can't be duplicated any other way.

- Improve Your Memory—People always think they will remember things, but if you've ever gone to the grocery store without a list, you know this is simply untrue. When we write something down we are much more likely to remember it, and if we don't, we can always go back and read it again.

Effective Journaling

Here are three simple steps to get started with journaling or improve your current journaling process.

Step One: Choose a format: physical or digital. You'll want to decide up front if you prefer a traditional, physical journal or a digital journal (on your computer or an app for your phone or tablet). If you aren't sure, experiment with both and see which feels best.

Step Two: Get a journal. Almost anything can work, but when it comes to a physical journal, there is something to be said for an attractive, durable one that you enjoy looking at—after all, ideally you're going to have it for the rest of your life. I like to buy nice leather journals with lines on the pages, but it's your journal, so choose what works best for you. Some people prefer journals without lines so they can draw or create mind maps. Others like to have one page for each day of the year that is predated to help them stay accountable.

Here are a few favorite physical journals from TMM Facebook Community:

- *The Five Minute Journal* has become popular among top performers. It has a very specific format for each day with prompts, such as "I am grateful for ..." and "What would make today great?" It takes five minutes or less and includes an evening option so you can review your day. (IntelligentChange.com)

- *The Miracle Morning Journal* is designed specifically to enhance and support your Miracle Morning by keeping you organized and accountable and to track your Life S.A.V.E.R.S. each day. You can download a free sample of *The Miracle Morning Journal* today at TMMbook.com to make sure it's right for you. (Amazon.com or MiracleMorningJournal.com)

- *The Plan: Your Legendary Life Planner* was designed by friends of ours, and it is a goal setting and habit tracking system and planner for people who are ready for life balance and are willing to be intentional about achieving level 10 in all areas of life. (LegendaryLifePlan.com)

If you prefer to use a digital journal, many choices are available. Here are a few favorites:

The Five Minute Journal also offers an iPhone app that follows the same format as the physical version and sends helpful reminders to make your entries each morning and evening. It also allows you to upload photos to create visual memories. (IntelligentChange.com)

- Day One is a popular journaling app, and it's perfect if you don't want any structure or any limits on how much you write. Day One offers a blank page, so if you like to write lengthy journal entries, this may be the app for you. (DayOneApp. com)

- Penzu is a popular online journal, which doesn't require an iPhone, iPad, or Android device. All you need is a computer. (Penzu.com)

Again, it really comes down to your preference and the features you want. Type "online journal" into Google or "journal" into the app store, and you'll get a variety of choices.

Step Three: Write daily. There are endless things you can write about in your journal. Notes on what you are reading, a gratitude list. Google "journal prompts" and write something completely different each day. You can record your favorite memories from the previous day, funny stories, or cute things your children said that you want to remember. Write whatever makes you feel good and don't worry about grammar, spelling, or punctuation. Your journal is a place to let your imagination run wild; so don't edit—just write!

Customizing the Life S.A.V.E.R.S.

I know that, as parents, you might have days when you can't do the Miracle Morning practice all at once. Feel free to split up the Life S.A.V.E.R.S. in any way that works for you and include your kids in your practice as well. I'll share more about this later, but here is an example. If your kids are old enough to meditate with you, invite them to join you. But if they're too young, it's probably best to practice silence by yourself. When mine were babies, I would do my Silence while nursing or rocking them to sleep.

I want to share a few ideas specifically geared toward customizing the Life S.A.V.E.R.S. based on your schedule and preferences. Your current morning routine might allow you to fit in only a 6-, 20-, or 30-minute Miracle Morning, or you might choose to do a longer version on the weekends.

Here is an example of a fairly common 60-minute Miracle Morning schedule using the Life S.A.V.E.R.S.

Silence: 10 minutes

Affirmations: 5 minutes

Visualization: 5 minutes

Exercise: 10 minutes

Reading: 20 minutes

Scribing: 10 minutes

You can customize the sequence, too. I prefer to do my reading and scribing first because it takes the most focus, which is hard to come by if I'm interrupted by our kids. Some parents prefer to do exercise first to get their blood pumping and wake themselves up, or like me, you might prefer to do exercise as your last activity in the Life S.A.V.E.R.S. so you're not sweaty during your Miracle Morning. Hal prefers to start with a period of peaceful, purposeful silence so that he can wake up slowly, clear his mind, and focus his energy and intentions. However, this is your Miracle Morning, not ours—feel free to experiment with different sequences to see which you like best.

Monica Dix, a mom in the Miracle Morning Community who is breastfeeding her baby, customizes her routine by getting out of the room as quickly and quietly as she can. The night before, she puts her clothes, toothbrush, and everything else she needs in another room. She effectively uses her baby as an alarm clock when the baby wakes between 3:00 and 6:00 a.m. She feeds the baby, and once her little one is back asleep, she does her one-hour Miracle Morning and then goes back to sleep herself. She recommends reading *Sweet Sleep: Nighttime and Naptime Strategies for the Breastfeeding Family* by Diane Wiessinger, Diana West, Linda J. Smith, and Teresa Pitman. It helped her understand how to incorporate her Miracle Morning into healthy sleep practices for her and the baby.

Ego Depletion and Your Miracle Morning

Have you ever wondered why you can resist sugary snacks in the morning, but your resistance crumbles in the afternoon or evening? Why is it that sometimes our willpower is strong and other times it deserts us? It turns out that willpower is like a muscle that grows tired from use, and at the end of the day, it is harder to push ourselves to do activities that serve us and avoid those that don't. It also means we have less patience for our loved ones in the afternoon and evening when they could probably use it the most.

The good news is that we know how this works and can set ourselves up for success with some advanced planning. And the great news? The Miracle Morning is an integral part of your plan. To see how this works, we need to understand ego depletion.

Ego depletion is a term to describe "a person's diminished capacity to regulate their thoughts, feelings, and actions," according to Roy F. Baumeister and John Tierney, the authors of *Willpower*. Ego depletion grows worse at the end of the day and when we are hungry, tired, or have had to exert our willpower too often.

If you wait until the end of the day to do important things that give you energy and help you become the person and parent you want to be, you'll find that your excuses are more compelling and your motivation has gone missing. But, when you wake up and do your Miracle Morning first thing, you gain the increased energy and mindfulness that the Life S.A.V.E.R.S. provide and keep ego depletion from getting in your way.

When you perform the Life S.A.V.E.R.S. habit every day, you learn the mechanics of habit formation when your willpower is strongest, and you can use this knowledge and energy to adopt small and doable habits at other times of the day.

Final Thoughts on the Life S.A.V.E.R.S.

Everything is difficult before it's easy. Every new experience is uncomfortable before it's comfortable. The more you practice the Life S.A.V.E.R.S., the more natural and normal each of them will feel. Hal's first time meditating was almost his last because his mind raced like a Ferrari, and his thoughts bounced around uncontrollably like the silver sphere in a pinball machine. Now, he loves meditation, and while he's still no master, he says he's decent at it.

Similarly, I had trouble with affirmations when I first started my Miracle Mornings. I didn't know what I wanted to affirm. So, I stole a few from *The Miracle Morning* and added a few that came to mind. It was okay, but they didn't really *mean* much to me initially. Over time, as I encountered things that struck me as powerful, I added them to my affirmations and adjusted the ones I had. Now, my affirmations mean a lot to me, and the daily act of using them is far more powerful.

In fact, I used the affirmation, "I am fully committed to writing *The Miracle Morning for Parents and Families* this year by sticking to my deadlines and protecting time to write" to motivate myself daily to finish this very book!

I invite you to begin practicing the Life S.A.V.E.R.S. now, so you can become familiar and comfortable with each of them and get a jump-start before you begin The Miracle Morning 30-Day Challenge in chapter 2.

If your biggest concern is still finding time, don't worry. I've got you covered. You can actually do the entire Miracle Morning—receiving the full benefits of all six Life S.A.V.E.R.S. in only six minutes a day! Simply do each of the Life S.A.V.E.R.S. for one minute: close your eyes and enjoy a moment of silence, visualize an achieved single action that you want to mentally practice for the day, say your affirmations (or repeat your favorite affirmation over and over). Next do jumping jacks, push-ups, or crunches. Grab a book and read a paragraph then jot down a few thoughts in your journal.

These six minutes will set you on the right path for the day—and you can always devote more time later when your schedule permits or the opportunity presents itself. Doing the six-minute practice is a way to start a mini habit to build up your confidence or a way to bookmark the habit on a tough morning. Say the baby woke up three times to feed in the night, and you didn't get much sleep, or you woke up with a pounding headache or fever. These are days for the six-minute practice (once the habit is formed). You will feel better for having done something, and it will hold the habit so you don't feel like you have to start all over when you feel better. Another mini habit you could do is to start with one of the Life S.A.V.E.R.S., and once you get used to waking up earlier, add more of them. Remember that the goal is to have some time to work on your personal goals and mindset, so if you are overwhelmed, it's not going to work for you.

Personally, my Miracle Morning has grown into a daily ritual of renewal and inspiration that I absolutely love! In the coming chapters, I will cover *a lot* of information that has the potential to turn you into a truly confident parent, and I can't wait to share it with you.

—4—

NOT-SO-OBVIOUS PARENTING PRINCIPLE #1:
SELF-LEADERSHIP

Parents are teachers, guides, leaders, protectors and providers for their children.
—Iyanla Vanzant, talk show host, inspirational speaker, and author of *Peace from Broken Pieces*

From the day they are born, our kids are watching us and learning about their world through our actions. They pick up language just by hearing us speak and are incredibly perceptive. As a parent, you are your child's first and, I'd dare to say, most important role model.

If our job as parents is to lead our children to become successful adults, then this starts with self-leadership. To help them grow and learn, we must do so first. To create the family we desire and deserve, we must master the key principles of self-leadership.

Andrew Bryant, founder of Self-Leadership International, summed it up this way: "Self-leadership is the practice of intentionally influencing your thinking, feeling, and behaviors to achieve your objective(s) ... [It] is having a developed sense of who you are, what you can do, and where you are going coupled with the ability to influence your communication, emotions, and behaviors on the way to getting there."

Before I reveal the key principles of self-leadership, I want to share with you what I've discovered about the crucial role that *mindset* plays as the foundation of effective self-leadership. Your past beliefs, self-image, and the ability to collaborate with and rely upon others at integral times will factor into your ability to excel as a self-leader.

Be Aware of—and Skeptical of—Your Self-Imposed Limitations

You may be holding on to false limiting beliefs that are subconsciously interfering with your ability to achieve your parenting goals.

For example, you may be someone who repeats, "I wish I were more organized" or "I wish I were better with math so I could help the kids understand their homework." Yet in reality, you are more than capable of providing the structure and inspiration to motivate the kids to do their work. Thinking of yourself as less than capable assumes imminent failure and simultaneously thwarts your ability to succeed. Life contains enough obstacles without your creating more for yourself!

Effective self-leaders closely examine their beliefs, decide which ones serve them, and eliminate the ones that don't.

When you find yourself stating anything that sounds like a limiting belief, from "I don't have enough time" to "I could never do that," pause and turn your self-limiting statements into empowering questions, such as the following: *Where can I find more time in my schedule? How might I be able to do that?*

Doing this allows you to tap into your inborn creativity and find solutions. You can always find a way when you're committed. As tennis star Martina Navratilova said, "The difference between involvement and commitment is like ham and eggs. The chicken is involved; the pig is committed." Being all in is the key to making anything happen.

See Yourself as Better than You've Ever Been

As Hal wrote in *The Miracle Morning*, most of us suffer from Rearview Mirror Syndrome, limiting our current and future results based on who we were in the past. Remember that, although *where you are is a result of who you were, where you go depends entirely on the person you choose to be from this moment forward.* This is especially important for parents. You will make mistakes with your children. Don't let your sense of guilt about that keep you from looking forward. Learn from your mistakes, and do better next time.

When we can model this for our kids, there is a much better chance that they will do the same. I watched an interview with Sara Blakely, the founder of Spanx, who is the youngest self-made female billionaire in the United States. She attributes her success to a mindset her father instilled in her. "When I was growing up, he encouraged us to fail. We'd come home from school and at dinner he'd say: 'What did you fail at today?' And if there was nothing, he'd be disappointed. It was a really interesting kind of reverse psychology. I would come home and say that I tried out for something and I was just horrible and he high-fived me." If we allow them to be, our mistakes can turn into our greatest lessons.

We all make mistakes! Human beings do not come with instructions, and children can be highly unpredictable. There will always be someone with an unsolicited opinion about the way you are raising your children. Don't listen to the static! Be confident in your choices as a parent, and when you aren't sure, find the answers and support you need. There is so much shaming of parents these days from "the mommy wars" to the "vigilante parenting" trend and online bullying. It saddens my heart. We need to find our compassion for people and put ourselves in their shoes before we judge their choices.

You do hear horrible stories about parents that intentionally harm their children. I think the media tends to exaggerate. For the most part, these things are true: parents want the best for their children, everyday parenting is not a life-or-death situation, and children are very resilient. I've made countless mistakes as a parent, and both of my children are thankfully still breathing.

When Tyler was a brand new baby, probably two weeks old or so, I noticed he was scratching his face. I decided it must be time to cut his fingernails for the first time. I got out the tiny clippers someone gave me in a baby shower gift and got started. The first nail was a success! The next nail, however, was not. Instead of clipping his fingernail, I accidentally clipped his finger. He immediately started screaming in pain as the blood flowed from the cut. I felt like the worst parent in the world at that moment, and in my sleep-deprived state, I started crying myself. Thankfully my mom was visiting us and came to my aid. She calmed me down and forced me to go take a nap. All parents make mistakes (especially when we are tired or not paying attention), but if you can learn to extract the lesson from the mistake, you will become a better parent for it—an exceptional parent.

The lessons I learned that day were:

- Accidents happen.

- Parental love won't protect my children from getting hurt, physically or emotionally.

- I sometimes will cause their pain unintentionally.

- Getting enough rest is important, and naps help.

I also realized that kids are resilient, cuts heal, emotional hurts can be overcome, and pain is often where our best lessons come from. After a little research, I also found that it's better to file a newborn's nails and not use clippers. That next day I saw myself as a better parent because of the ordeal.

All successful parents, at some point, made the choice to see themselves as better than they had ever been before. They stopped maintaining limiting beliefs based on their past and instead started forming beliefs based on their unlimited potential. We also need to see our children in this light. Truly, our kids have the same unlimited potential, yet we are often the ones who limit them with *our* fears or the guilt we project onto them.

Here's a story from our friend Jon Vroman, founder of the Front Row Foundation, about his son Tiger. Jon took four-year-old Tiger to a carnival where he saw a 40-foot climbing wall, and right away Tiger wanted to climb it. Jon was apprehensive because he didn't want his son to be disappointed when he couldn't make it to the top. Jon tried to steer him to a different ride, but after Tiger's persistence, Jon let him give it a try.

Tiger eagerly got harnessed up and started ascending while a carnival worker held his rope. He had climbed about 30 feet up when the wall began to bend outward, making it more challenging. Jon thought for sure his son couldn't make it to the top, and almost on cue, Tiger looked down and said, "Papa, I can't."

Jon looked up and said, "It's okay, buddy, you tried."

The man working for the carnival turned to Jon and said, "I think your boy can make it," and then shouted up to Tiger, "Hey buddy, try again!" With his newfound confidence and a little encouragement, he tried one more time.

Tiger climbed all the way to the top and hit a button that caused lights to flash and a huge smile to spread across his face. In that moment Jon, a well-known life coach and motivational speaker, felt elated for Tiger yet horrible as a father. Why was it so easy for the man working at the carnival to see Tiger's potential but not Jon? Because Jon was suffering from Rearview Mirror Syndrome. Jon realized that he was seeing Tiger for what he used to be and not for what Tiger was now or even what he could be in the future. Once he realized his mistake, he was able to change his mindset and use this experience to help other people. Even a well-known motivational speaker needs a lesson in how to motivate his child every now and then.

One of the best ways to see yourself as a better parent each day is to follow the four-step formula for creating affirmations outlined in chapter 3. Be sure to create affirmations that reinforce what's possible for you and remind you of whom you're committed to becoming. Your affirmations will evolve over time, so experiment with different types until you find what resonates with you the most.

Actively Seek Support

As the old adage says, it takes a village to raise a child. Seeking support is crucial for parents, yet many struggle, suffering in silence because they assume everyone else has greater capabilities, and they all but refuse to seek help and assistance.

Parents who are self-leaders know they can't do it alone. You might need moral support, for example, so you can replenish the energy stores that kids are so famous for depleting. Or you may need accountability support to overcome your tendency to disengage when the going gets tough. We all need support in different areas of our lives, and great self-leaders understand that and use it to their benefit.

The Miracle Morning Community on Facebook is a great place to start looking for support. The members are positive and responsive. Try joining a local parents group in your area. Meetup.com is a great place to find like-minded parents who are close by. I highly recommend getting an accountability partner and, if you can, a life coach to help you.

I also think it is vitally important for kids to be exposed to viewpoints from people other than mom and dad. If you have family close by, lean on them for support. I am blessed to have my parents only 15 minutes away, and they love to spend time with their grandchildren! They sometimes call us to ask to babysit. You may not have the same situation, but *anything* is possible when you are committed. You could start a babysitting co-op with friends or neighbors, hire a babysitter or mother's helper in your neighborhood, or find another creative solution. Many gyms, churches, and children's activity centers have date nights where you can drop your kids off for a few hours of fun and pizza while the parents go out for a night on the town.

The Five Core Principles of Self-Leadership

To grow personally and become an exceptional mom or dad, you'll need to become a remarkable self-leader. My favorite way to cut the learning curve in half and decrease the time it takes for you to improve your parenting skills is to look for people whose relationships with their children you admire and use them as role models.

In researching this book, I've read many books on mindset that reveal a multitude of effective strategies. Here are the five I believe will shave years off your pursuit of self-leadership excellence:

1. Take 100 Percent Responsibility
2. Become Financially Free
3. Put Fitness First
4. Systematize Your World
5. Commit to Consistency

Principle #1: Take 100 Percent Responsibility

Here's the hard truth: If you're not living the life and achieving the goals you want right now, it's all on you. That being said, your children's behavior and choices should not determine your success as a parent. Our kids are separate beings, and they must be on their own path and make their own mistakes to learn their lessons. If your toddler has a meltdown in the grocery store, it does not mean you are a terrible parent, but how you handle that situation is important, and for that you need to take 100 percent responsibility. We do also have to consider that our kids are young people. If we did not feed said toddler and she has a meltdown at the grocery store, then we need to take 100 percent responsibility for that meltdown. We are the adult in the situation and should act accordingly.

The sooner you take responsibility, the sooner you'll begin to move forward. This isn't meant to be harsh. It's meant as a wake-up call. The most successful people in the world are rarely victims; they take absolute responsibility for everything in their lives, whether it's their fault or not, personal or professional, good or bad, their job or someone else's.

While mediocre parents complain often but do nothing to improve their situations, successful parents look at their own individual role in every situation and analyze how they could be better. They find the right resources, and more importantly, they intentionally seek to acquire the skills necessary to build healthy family relationships that are so important in raising children.

According to Hal, "The moment you take 100 percent responsibility for *everything* in your life is the same moment you claim the power to change *anything* in your life. But you must understand that responsibility is not the same thing as blame. Blame determines who is at fault for something; responsibility determines who is committed to improving a situation. It rarely matters who is at fault; what matters is that YOU are committed to improving your situation." He's right. And it's so empowering when you act accordingly. Suddenly, life is in your control.

When you take true ownership of your life, there's no time to discuss who's at fault. If you own your results, you make them happen. You always have a choice about how you respond in any situation.

Here's an example. You're on the way to the gym with the kids in tow when you hit a pothole and damage your tire. You could waste your time blaming the city for not fixing it and cursing them (victim mentality), or you could demonstrate self-control and take action to fix the problem. You can snap at the service workers when they finally show up to help you get to the shop, or you can treat them with respect and understanding. You can let that event ruin your day, or you can treat it like an adventure.

As Ryland Engelhart, chief visionary officer at Café Gratitude, has said, "Our true RESPONSE-ability is our ability to respond."

When we blame our children because we are not living the life we want, it leads to resentment, which can create a toxic household environment. Even if it was not your intention or choice to have a child, it's time to take responsibility for your life and your children. Blaming them for any unfulfilled dream is not fair, and pushing them to live your dream is worse. Own your dreams, and find a way to make them reality for *yourself.*

Principle #2: Aim to Become Financially Free and Act Accordingly

According to the USDA, the average cost of raising a child born in 2013 (tinyurl.com/p8h5l7n) through age 18 for a middle-income family in the US is approximately $245,340, which is about $12,800–$14,970 per year. And that is before they get to college! How is your financial situation? Are you earning significantly more money each month than you need to survive? Are you able to save, invest, and share part of your income regularly?

If not, don't be too hard on yourself; you're not alone. The majority of people have less than $10,000 to their name and an average of $16,000 in unsecured debt. No judgment here if this describes you; I'm simply going to point you back to Principle #1 and encourage you to take 100 percent responsibility for your financial situation. We've seen and heard every reason for someone to dive deep into debt, fail to save, and not have a nest egg. None of those matter now. Yes, the best time to have started saving a percentage of your income was 5, 10, or even 20 years ago. But the next best time is right now. Whether you're 20, 40, or 60 years old, it's never too late to take control of your personal finances. You'll find an incredible boost in energy from taking charge, and you'll be able to use your accumulated savings to create even more wealth because you'll actually have money to invest in new opportunities. Sounds good, right?

It's more important than ever to pay attention to finances, both in making more money, if possible, and being smart about what you do with it. It turns out that learning how to make money is only half the battle. Learning how to *keep* it by saving and investing wisely is a large part of the puzzle.

Financial freedom isn't something you achieve overnight. It is a result of developing the mindset and the habits *now* that will take you down the path that leads to financial freedom. It has nothing to do with how much money you make. It's all about living within your means, learning how money works, and finding investment vehicles that allow your money to work for you. If you follow a budget and keep your expenses low, the power of compound interest will eventually grow your passive income to a level where it covers or exceeds your cost of living. Financial freedom is achievable for anyone who is willing to do the work and become a student of money.

Here are the three steps you can do right now to get you started on the path:

Step One: Set aside 10 percent of your income to save and invest. In fact, I recommend that you start by taking 10 percent of whatever you have in the bank right now and putting it in a savings account. (Go ahead, I'll wait.) Make whatever adjustments you need to make to your lifestyle to live off of 90 percent of your current income.

Said another way, pay yourself first. Think of your savings account as money for your future. Pay that account first, and then live off the rest, not the other way around. Most people pay all their bills, and if anything happens to be left over, they save it. Guess what? Nothing will ever be left over with that strategy! Put 10 percent aside first and then live off the rest. If that means the cable bill doesn't get paid, that's ok. Make a list of your priorities and values, and if something does not fit into those, stop paying for it to ensure you will have money to save. For example, if one of your family values is to be healthy, but you're spending hundreds on eating fast food each month, it may be time to reevaluate that expense.

For us, saving is automated. We've set up an automatic transfer twice a month for 10 percent of our paychecks to go into a savings account. This way we are not tempted to spend that money. I've heard of people going so far as to have their savings at a different bank that they can access only by going into the branch to make a withdraw. Saving is that important!

Step Two: Take another 10 percent and give it away. Most wealthy people give a percentage of their income to causes they believe in. But you don't have to wait until you're wealthy to start this practice. Tony Robbins said, "If you won't give $1 out of $10, you'll never give $1 million out of $10 million." Can't do 10 percent or the rent check will bounce? Fine, start with 5, 2, or 1 percent. It's not the amount that matters, but developing the mindset and creating the habit that will change your financial future and serve you for the rest of your life. If money is too tight at the moment, give your time or your skills instead. You've got to start teaching your subconscious brain that you can produce an abundant income, that there's more than enough, and that more is always on the way. This mindset is an important one for you and your kids. They are watching how you handle your finances. Show them how to create abundance, and they'll thank you for the rest of their lives.

To teach our kids about money, we give them each an allowance (yes even our three-year-old gets one). They make $15 a week, but they have to split it up. They get $7 to spend, $5 to save, and $3 to donate. Once they save $50, we take them to the bank to deposit it in their savings account where it gains interest. Anytime they come across a cause they want to support, they can take money from their donation envelope. So far our kids have given money to 1LifeFul-lyLived.org, Turkeybundance.org (a Thanksgiving turkey drive), and our local hospital's foundation. We talk to them about money and introduce them to basic money principles like interest and the idea of investing.

We do not tie their allowance to any specific behavior. But we do expect them to be productive and contributing members of the family, and in exchange for that, they receive money that we expect them to manage according to our family values. This helps them to understand how money works and to take responsibility for attracting it and making sound choices for its use. We realize that young kids will make plenty of mistakes with their money, but it's much better to learn those lessons early then to be overwhelmed when they have to decide to go into debt to pay for college.

In his book, *The Opposite of Spoiled: Raising Kids Who Are Grounded, Generous, and Smart About Money*, Ron Lieber says, "Every conversation about money is also about values. Allowance is also about patience. Giving is about generosity. Work is about perseverance. Negotiating their wants and needs and the difference between the two has a lot to do with thrift and prudence." Teaching your kids about money is also teaching them your family values, so don't give them the silent treatment.

Step Three: Continuously educate yourself on the topic of money. Now that you have kids, it's one of the most important topics for you to master, and you can start by adding the following books, which cover various aspects of financial freedom, to your reading list:

- *Rich Dad Poor Dad: What The Rich Teach Their Kids About Money That the Poor and Middle Class Do Not!* by Robert Kiyosaki

- *MONEY Master the Game: 7 Simple Steps to Financial Freedom* by Tony Robbins

- *Secrets of the Millionaire Mind: Mastering the Inner Game of Wealth* by T. Harv Eker

- *The Total Money Makeover: A Proven Plan for Financial Fitness* by Dave Ramsey

- *The Millionaire Fastlane: Crack the Code to Wealth and Live Rich for a Lifetime* by MJ DeMarco

- *The Opposite of Spoiled: Raising Kids Who are Grounded, Generous, and Smart About Money* by Ron Lieber

- *The First National Bank of Dad: The Best Way to Teach Kids About Money* by David Owen

- *Earn It, Learn It: Teach Your Child the Value of Money, Work, and Time Well Spent* by Alisa T. Weinstein

Principle #3: Put Fitness First

How's your health these days? Can you wake up before your alarm and do what's important, handle all the demands of the day, and put out the inevitable fires without ending the day exhausted and out of breath?

We discussed exercise as part of the Life S.A.V.E.R.S., and yes, I'm going to talk about it again right now. It's a fact that the state of your health and fitness are huge factors in your energy and success levels—especially for parents. Responding with compassion to the steady stream of needs, crises, school projects, social dilemmas, and last-minute requests that your children throw at you requires a ton of energy. Parenting truly is an energy sport. Like any sport, you need an almost endless supply of energy and stamina.

To be available for advice, meal making, fun conversation, emotional support, physical play, art projects, and clean up—I could go on here, but the list would be as long as the rest of the book—can be exhausting. If you are overweight, out of shape, and constantly out of breath, setting higher parenting goals for yourself is, in my opinion, a recipe for disaster. You will feel as if there's more day than there is energy.

The great news is that this is (almost) completely within your control!

Here are three practices of healthy parents that you can use to ensure that your health, fitness, and energy levels fully support your parenting goals and objectives:

1. Eat and drink to win. Put very simply, everything you ingest either contributes to your health or detracts from it. Drinking water puts a check in the plus column; double shots of tequila won't. Eating fresh fruits and vegetables equals more plusses. Rolling through the drive-through to wolf down some fast food? Not so much. I know you know the drill. This isn't rocket science, but you do need to stop fooling yourself. Today, I encourage you to become aware of what you're eating and how it affects your life. I'll dive deeper into this in the next chapter, Energy Engineering. But let me also point out the obvious: Your kids watch how you handle food. You know you want your kids to live healthy lives. That's not even a question. But you need to show them how. And the time to start doing that is today.

2. Sleep to win. I want to say this as a gentle reminder: A good night's sleep provides the basis for a day of peak energy levels, clear thought, and successful decision making. You probably already know how many hours you need to be at your best, and believe me, you'll get back to that schedule eventually. But don't give up trying either, even if your kids wake you up 10 times a night. As much as possible, reverse engineer your schedule so you are asleep in plenty of time to get all the rest you need to perform at your best. And if you are home during the day with the kids, pay attention to their sleep cycles and manage them to afford the kids and yourself the best night's sleep possible. And when you can, nap when they do!

3. Exercise to win. It is no coincidence that you rarely see energetic parents who are terribly out of shape. Most invest 30–60 minutes of their time each day to hit the gym or the running trail because they understand the important role that daily exercise plays in their success. And while the E in the Life S.A.V.E.R.S. ensures that you start each day with 5–10 minutes of exercise, I recommended that you engage in 30–60 minute workouts at least three to five times per week. Doing so will ensure that your fitness level supports the energy and confidence you need to be a great parent.

Principle #4: Systematize Your World

Effective self-leaders have *systems* for just about everything from work activities, such as scheduling, follow up, entering orders, and sending thank you cards to personal activities, such as sleeping, eating, managing money, cars, and family responsibilities. Those systems make life easier and ensure parents are ready for anything.

Here are three examples of basic techniques:

1. Automate What You Can—In our household milk is a necessity. We constantly had to stop at the grocery store for another gallon, and it became burdensome. We discovered that a local farm still delivers milk the old-fashioned way, so we decided to have our milk delivered to us instead of running out all the time for more. If you find something in your life that does not bring you joy, try to eliminate it through automation.

I hate cleaning toilets and doing the laundry. So I found a way to hire help for those chores. One benefit of that is that it makes us accountable for keeping the house clutter free. The cleaners can do their job well only if things are up off the floor and surfaces. Tuesday night in our house is pick up time. The whole family gets involved to get the house ready for the cleaners. I realize house cleaners may not be in the budget for every family, but if you can't afford a house cleaner, you may be able to trade services with friends or come up with other creative solutions. One mom I know includes house cleaning as the exercise portion of the Life S.A.V.E.R.S. So a little gets done every morning.

2. Diaper Bags and Beyond—Hal, in addition to being a best-selling author, is a speaker who travels week after week, sharing *The Miracle Morning* message with audiences around the country and abroad. Collecting the items he needed for every trip was time-consuming, inefficient, and ineffective because he would often forget something at home or in his office. After the third time he forgot the charger for his computer and had to find an Apple store to buy a $99 replacement (ouch) or ask the front desk for a phone charger, shaver, or an extra set of cufflinks left behind by a previous guest, he'd had enough. He assembled a travel bag containing every item he needs for his trips, and now he can leave at a moment's notice because his bag contains everything to conduct business on the road: business cards, brochures, copies of his books, adapters, and chargers for his phone and computer. He even includes earplugs in case his hotel room neighbor is noisy.

You'll know you need a system when you have a recurring challenge or find that you're missing important items because you're unprepared. If you're walking out the door with just enough time to get to your first destination of the day on schedule only to discover your car is running on fumes, you need a system for getting out the door earlier. Here are some ways to plan ahead:

- pack your kids' lunches and your gym bag the night before
- keep a bag in the car with a change of clothes for when the kids inevitably get wet or dirty
- prepare a first-aid kit with sunscreen, Band-Aids, bug spray, and wet wipes

- stash healthy snacks for when you're on the go (apples, kale chips, carrots, etc.) to prevent stopping at a convenience store for a not-so-healthy option

Said another way, wherever you need to get your act together, you need a system. A life without systems is a life with unnecessary stress! This is especially true for busy parents.

3. Flexible Time Blocking—I am going to share something with you that will totally change your ability to produce consistent and spectacular results with your kids. Many of you may even want to slap yourselves when you hear this because it is something that almost all parents know and almost none of them do effectively on a consistent basis: *You must have a predetermined action plan filled with the activities that will get you to your chosen goals. Then put all the activities into a time-blocked daily schedule and live by it as much as is humanly possible.*

Children thrive on a schedule, and the more predictable their routines are, the more secure they will feel. That's not to say you cannot have flexibility in your schedule. In fact, I strongly suggest that you plan plenty of leeway, especially if you have young children. When you use time blocking, achieving your goals is no longer a matter of *if*, but only a matter of *when*.

How many times has your child failed to put their shoes on after you've asked them three times to do it and then you are late to your first destination? Chances are, you get more behind as the day goes on, and by the end of the day very little on your to-do list has been accomplished. Mike is able to time block more traditionally because he needs to for work, but as a full-time stay-at-home mom, I need to add more flexibility for the kids. Kids get sick, they have bad dreams, and they aren't always hungry when it's time to eat before they have to get to school, so I have a general schedule I follow instead of rigid blocks.

I follow what I call my ideal week. Every day is a little different with my current schedule, so that's why it's the ideal week instead of the ideal day. For example, here is my ideal Monday:

- 6:30 wake up and do Miracle Morning
- 7:30–8:45 kids wake, and we get ready for the day
- 8:45 leave for school

- Next go to the gym while Tyler's in school and Ember is in on-site childcare

- After the gym, go to the grocery store with Ember and eat lunch there

- When we get home, put the groceries away and put the Ember down for a nap

- Have about two hours to tackle to-do list

- Kids are up or home (allow some screen time if needed for more to-dos) or enjoy playtime with the kids

- 5:30 start dinner with help from the kids

- Eat when dinner is ready

- Clean up from dinner while Mike spends time with the kids

- 8:00 all electronics turned off, bath or quiet time, reading, and sleep

- After kids are asleep, spend time with Mike then go to bed

You will notice some things have an actual time assigned, while others are event driven: do this, then this, and then this. I've included the *ideal* schedule, and this approach requires a separate planning system where to-dos are listed (preferably in order of priority, so you tackle the most crucial first).

I also keep mental notes of how long things take during the day. For example, it takes the kids about 10 minutes to find and get their shoes on before we can get out the door, so if we need to leave at 8:45 to be somewhere, I know that by at least 8:35 I have to ask the kids to start that process. I also have to be flexible if something unexpected comes up. For example, if my daughter wakes up with a fever when I had planned to take her with me to the gym to get a workout in, I have to shift gears. Since that is no longer a possibility, I do my workout when my daughter is down for her nap instead.

Here's another example: I know it takes about two hours to go to the grocery store, do the shopping, and get home. If on the way to the grocery store, Ember complains that she is tired, I take her home for a nap and tackle some items on my to-do list. I do the shopping after she's rested. I can simply switch the time blocks for the nap and grocery store. In his book *The ONE Thing*, Gary Keller, the founder of Keller Williams Realty International, says this: "Sometimes the request is real, needs to be done now, and you must follow the rule, 'If you erase, you must replace' and immediately reschedule your time block." A tired preschooler, in my opinion, cannot be ignored. It's much better to take her home to get rested and reschedule the grocery store visit for later that day.

Anything that is already automated gets plugged into the ideal week too, so part of Tuesday after dinner cleanup is to pick up the house. And Wednesday includes the cleaners.

There's no need to reinvent the wheel to create a system. Chances are, someone has struggled with and overcome any challenge you face. Look for these people online or in your community. If ideas escape you, find the closest person who excels at what you struggle with and ask their advice! They may be on the same path as you, just a little farther ahead. Soon, you'll have the systems you need and the extra energy they provide.

Principle #5: Commit to Consistency

If there is any not-so-obvious secret to success, this is it: *Commit to consistency*. Every result that you desire—from improving your physique to increasing the size of your business to spending more quality time with your family—requires a consistent approach to produce the desired results.

Parental consistency has been linked to fewer behavioral problems in kids. "Consistency between parents and caregivers is very important," says Bernard Arons, M.D., director of the Center for Mental Health Services, in Washington, DC. "A child learns how to approach the world by observing the behavior and values of the people around him. The more consistent the messages he gets, the more stable he feels. Without consistency, kids have a hard time controlling themselves." Research has shown that an authoritative approach is the most effective. In other words, parents and caregivers who encourage kids to keep commitments, think for themselves, and consider the reasons for the rules offer both freedom and responsibility to their children.

Parents who inspire consistent behavior in their children simply take consistent action themselves. For example, if the rule is no screen time until the kids are dressed and have eaten breakfast, but one morning that rule suddenly goes out the window, it's confusing for the kids. You can't insist that your children follow the rules only when you feel like enforcing them or only when you're inspired. You have to define your parenting expectations and family values and take consistent action, day in and day out, for an extended period so the kids adopt them and know what to expect.

So many parents read a parenting book, try the suggestions for a week, and decide that the approach doesn't work. They either revert to their natural parenting style or move on to the next book and try that for a week with little to no results. In our culture of instant gratification, we are so quick to decide something isn't working if we don't get immediate results. We do not give the process we choose any time to create the results we desire in our kids.

In the chapters that follow, I'll give you the insight and direction you need to take consistent action. For now, prepare your mind to keep going—even when the results you want aren't coming fast enough—and to have the stamina to withstand plenty of rejection and disappointment from your kids as they adjust to their new mom and dad. The best parents are consistent, persistent, and unfailing in their dedication to taking action every day, and you need to be the same!

How is Your Self-Esteem Doing?

As American playwright August Wilson suggests, "Confront the dark parts of yourself, and work to banish them with illumination and forgiveness. Your willingness to wrestle with your demons will cause your angels to sing." Self-esteem gives you the courage to try new things and the power to believe in yourself.

It is vitally important that you give yourself permission to feel proud of yourself. Yes, we need to be realistic about our weaknesses and always strive to improve, but don't hesitate to be proud of your strengths and revel in the little wins. Often parenting is a thankless job. When we impose limits on our kids for their benefit, they will not appreciate it until much later in life. In the meantime, many days are filled with complaints from the kids, so it is vitally important that you love yourself. If you are doing the best you can, give yourself credit. I keep a special section in my journal to write love notes to myself. On days I need a little extra encouragement, I write down all the things I love and appreciate about me.

An unstoppable self-esteem is a powerful tool. You probably already know that with a negative attitude you are going nowhere—and fast! With the right attitude, all the complaints from your kids can roll off your back. You stay calm and are able to connect with them on a deeper level. When you are confident in your abilities as a parent and committed to consistency, your behavior will change, and your kids will come along with you.

Final Thoughts on Self-Leadership

Let's review the concepts we discussed in this chapter. We talked about the importance of self-leadership in improving your family life. Developing self-leadership helps put you in the leadership role in your life as a whole. It eliminates the victim mentality and ensures you know the values, beliefs, and vision you want to impart to your children.

Step One: Review and integrate the Five Core Principles of Self-Leadership:

1. **Take 100 Percent Responsibility.** Remember, the moment you accept responsibility for *everything* in your life is the moment you claim the power to change *anything* in your life. Your success is 100 percent up to you.

2. **Become Financially Free.** Begin to develop the mindset and habits that will inevitably lead you to a life of financial freedom, including saving a minimum of 10 percent of your income and continuing to educate yourself on the topic of money.

3. **Put Fitness First.** If daily fitness isn't already a priority in your life, make it so. In addition to your morning exercise, block time for longer, 30- to 60-minute workouts three to five times each week.

4. **Systematize Your World.** Start putting systems and flexible time blocked schedules in place so that every day your processes have been predetermined and your success is virtually

guaranteed. It's then simply a matter of waking up and following through with what you've planned to do when you planned to do it.

5. **Commit to Consistency.** Children need structure. Choose consistency with your children and commit to family expectations and values. If you're trying a new approach, give it an extended period of time to work before throwing in the towel to try something different.

Step Two: Develop your self-control and upgrade your self-image by using affirmations and visualization. Be sure to customize both at your earliest opportunity—it takes time to see results, and the sooner you start, the sooner you'll notice improvements.

By now I hope you've gained a sense of how important your personal development is in creating a successful family. As you read this book—and I suggest you read it more than twice—I recommend that you intentionally address the areas where you know you need improvement and expansion. If your self-esteem could use a boost, then take steps to elevate it. Design affirmations to increase and develop it over time. Visualize yourself acting with more confidence, raising your personal standards, and loving yourself more.

If this sounds overwhelming, remember the power of incremental change. You don't have to do everything all at once. And, I've got more good news for you. In the next chapter, I'm going to tackle how to create more than enough energy to make these changes and be as successful as you want to be.

PARENTING PROFILE
Gary Keller

Gary is a New York Times best-selling author, real estate broker, and entrepreneur. He founded Keller Williams Realty International, the largest real estate franchise sales organization in the world with headquarters in Austin, Texas.

Gary is married with one son, age 24.

Parenting Philosophy

Ultimately, our character is what defines who we are. As parents, I believe our most important job is to help our child understand and decide who he wants to be. Self-image is a part of that. Skill set is a part of that. Standards are a part of that. Creating standards starts with the small things. You don't lie. You don't cheat. You keep your word. As a parent, it's important to set the tone of what the standards are going to be, so that at some point, your child opts in to those standards.

Best Parenting Tips

Put your family first. Probably, the simplest, most effective thing I did when our son was born was start putting all the personal things first on my calendar and then simply work in between. Literally, I plan my personal life first, and I block in all the key dates from the holidays to the birthdays to the vacations.

Be present. One thing that our son taught me early on is that you can't be with your child physically but mentally be somewhere else.

You can't be with your child playing dinosaur checkers and be thinking about business. That doesn't work. You have to be fully present. My philosophy became "wherever I am—be there."

Curate your child's relationships. As you're helping your child find out who he is, what he wants to do, and what he feels good about, the people your child spends time with are important. I began to realize that one of the tactics that I could use as a parent was to put the best people I could find in front of our son. I began to curate them. I began to look for really good, fun, coaches and teachers for him who also had good values, good standards, and good ethics. That way, our son was not only learning a skill, but was also getting parented by people he might listen to.

Make your house a Welcome House. Our goal was for our son's friends to feel like Mary and I were their second set of parents. So we made our house a Welcome Home. Today, our son's best friend doesn't even knock. He just walks in the house. We worked really hard for that.

Participate in individual sports. When our son was young, I could see the value of team sports and I encouraged our son to play them. However, one day I realized as cool as team sports are, those who played them when they were kids weren't playing them as an adult. The people that seemed to continue with their sport throughout their life were the ones who did individual sports. And more importantly to me, I noticed that the individual sports would be the ones we could do with our son for a lifetime. And that's how it worked out.

Build confidence. My observation is that the people who get the most out of life are the ones who have the most confidence. The question is how do you get confidence? I discovered we are either born with it or develop it. And since we didn't want to assume our son was born with it, we worked at helping him develop it. The way we approached it was to help him become good at something, and sure enough, that gave him confidence. That confidence then built on itself. The chain reaction of confidence building confidence building confidence is what we were working towards, and we believed that no accomplishment was too small to ignore.

Parenting Success Story

Direct your children. A lot of parents say, "I don't want to influence my kid. I want them to make their own decisions." But if you ask "Why is Bob Dylan's son a musician? Why is Tom Hanks's son an actor?" They made those decisions most likely because their parents pulled them into their world and helped them fall in love with it. I'd like to be in relationship with my son forever. I don't know what that looks like, but I decided I wanted to foster an understanding of business or some sort of affinity towards it to give us a fighting chance to be in business together someday. So I exposed him to books like *Rich Dad, Poor Dad* while he was growing up. My son eventually made the decision to be a businessman.

Final Word

Allow yourself to experience the joy. Children naturally feel joy, and that was one of the great gifts I got from being a parent. Kids just naturally behave with joy and find it in the simplest of things. As we get older, life somehow conspires to knock some of that joy out of us. I learned that there's nothing wrong with being joyful and that finding it somehow in everything we do is important. That's not always easy, but I've learned it's in there somewhere. It may be big or it may be tiny, but it's there. To know that it's there and find it is one of the great lessons I learned from being a parent.

PARENTING PROFILE
Honorée Corder

Honorée Corder is the author of 19 best-selling books, including The Successful Single Mom series.

Honorée was a single mom for seven years, is now re-married, and has one daughter, age 16.

Parenting Philosophy

Your children are on their own journey. I believe my job as a mom is to provide unconditional love and support for my daughter. Additionally, I'm providing the space for her to find her own way, make her own mistakes. I am there to listen and provide advice and counsel. As much as you might want something in particular for your kids, or for them to choose a certain path, it is ultimately our job as parents to equip them with the tools, skills, and problem-solving abilities they will need for their entire adult lives.

How has The Miracle Morning affected your parenting?

I have a dozen affirmations around how I am as a woman, the example I set for my daughter as a wife, business woman, friend, and of course as a mom. I visualize our daily interactions as being kind and loving, with maximum patience on my part. The Life S.A.V.E.R.S. have set the stage for me to have extreme personal and professional happiness, allowing for me to be at my best much more often than not. The daily practices set the stage for each day to be magical and miraculous, and when you have enough of those days in a row, your life (and therefore your parenting by default) becomes magical and miraculous.

Best [Single] Parenting Tips

Parenting has affected my life in every way! It has affected my language (what I say and don't say) and even my schedule (what time I go to bed so I can spend time with my daughter before school).

It doesn't seem like they are listening and watching, but they really are! I can't be the only mom who feels like I'm wasting my breath! But as my daughter has gotten older, I can see the results of both my great (and sometimes not-so-great) parenting. She has excellent manners because that was incredibly important to me—I wanted a child others would enjoy being around, who would be respectful and cheerful. I must have said, *Say please!* and *Say thank you!* a zillion times before I felt like she got it, but to this day she's incredibly polite and helpful. But I know that's because I am polite and helpful not because I told her to be so and then did something else. Your kids will do what you do not what you say (especially if they are incongruent).

One awesome parent is enough. Single parents tend to be very hard on themselves, and one worry I had, and have heard many times from others, is being a solo parent is an ingredient in their children's recipe for disaster in life. I absolutely disagree: I believe one terrific parent, especially one who is aware enough and conscious enough to engage in self-development, can and will raise incredible children who can impact the world in countless, positive ways.

Practice extreme self-care. The Life S.A.V.E.R.S. are important, especially for single parents, because they set a personal example for your children that you are important too. A parent who practices self-sacrifice for their children only lives to see those actions—and lack of actions—backfire. Taking excellent care of yourself will show your children that taking care of themselves isn't negotiable, and their overall health, happiness, and well-being is largely influenced by how well they do it!

Focus on what is truly important. Given the choice between unloading the dishwasher or doing laundry and spending time talking with, or reading to, or doing a fun activity with your kids, well, the chores can wait! While your kids won't remember their impeccable closets or a clean kitchen floor, they will remember when you looked them in the eyes and asked them about their day, or when you intentionally got off your phone to love on them while watching a movie together.

Final Word

I encourage all moms, single or married, to give themselves and those they love the gift of the Life S.A.V.E.R.S. There is no downside, only an incredible life that awaits you when you discover and become all you can be with the Miracle Morning.

— 5 —

NOT-SO-OBVIOUS PARENTING PRINCIPLE #2:
Energy-Engineering

I don't know what's more exhausting about parenting: the getting up early, or acting like you know what you're doing.
— Jim Gaffigan, Stand-up comedian and author of *Dad Is Fat*

When all goes well, parenting is wonderful. You have fun, you feel connected to your kids, everyone gets along with each other, and you have hope and feel you can take on the world.

The trouble is it isn't all up to you. On some days—and I know you've had those days—you wake up, and you just don't have the energy or motivation you need to meet the challenges you know are coming. Being a parent can be exhausting, both physically and mentally—and that's on the good days. Sometimes parenting involves uncertainty, rejection, refusal, and disappointment. The good days take energy, enthusiasm, and persistence. The hard days take all that and more.

Parenting requires an abundance of energy. There's no way around it. You can have the best kids, the best partner, and the best action plan for the day, but if you don't have the *energy* to take advantage of them, you might as well prepare for something to go wrong. If you want to maximize your time with your children, you need energy—the more the better, and the more *consistent* the better.

- Energy helps you be there for your kids day after day.

- Energy is contagious—it spreads from you to your family like a positive virus, creating symptoms of enthusiasm and yes responses everywhere.

- Energy is the foundation of everything.

- Energy is what determines the success we attract.

The question then becomes, how do you generate and maintain a high level of sustainable energy on demand?

When we struggle with energy issues, we might try to compensate with caffeine and other stimulants, and they'll work for a while … until we crash. You may have noticed the same thing.

If you've been fueling yourself on coffee and pure determination, you haven't even begun to reach the heights of achievement that are possible when you build and tap into the energy you have within you.

Natural Energy Cycles

The first thing to understand about energy is that the goal isn't to be running at full speed all the time. It isn't practical to maintain a constant output. As human beings, we have a natural ebb and flow to our energy levels. Parenting, it turns out, is the same. You may be tired in the morning, but your children are ready to go. Or you may be energized in the evenings, and your children are exhausted from their activities during the day. And we have patterns that arise during different times of the year as well. When school starts, children might feel excited or scared—both high-energy states. They may have a lot of homework or conflicts with other children to deal with, which they may or may not tell you about. And when summer vacation rolls around, you may need as much energy as you can get.

The trick is to marry, or at least try to sync up, your cycles with your children's. Observe your kids and make note of their rhythms. Know that you will need to access deeper wells of energy during particularly intense times throughout the year and allow yourself the time to rest, rejuvenate, and recharge when the intensity lessens.

One important thing that parents are prone to forget: Just like houseplants need water, our energy reserves need regular replenishing. You can go full tilt for long periods of time, but eventually your mind, body, and spirit will need to be refilled. Think of your life as a container that holds your energy. When you do not properly manage what's in your container, it's like having a hole in the bottom. No matter how much you pour in, you still won't feel fully energized.

Instead of letting yourself get to the point of being overwhelmed, burned out, or stressed out, why not become proactive about your energy levels and have an auto-recharge system in place? This will help you plug the holes in your container and allow you to fill up with the energy you need.

If you have resigned yourself to being tired, cranky, behind on your to-do list, out of shape, and unhappy, I have some great news.

Being continually exhausted is not only unacceptable, *you don't have to settle for it.* There are a few simple ways to get what you need and want—more rest, time to replenish and recharge, and inner peace and happiness. A tall order? Yes. Impossible? Heck, no!

This is about strategically engineering your life for optimum and sustainable physical, mental, and emotional energy, which will benefit you and your family. Here are the three principles I follow to keep my energy reserves at maximum capacity and on tap for whenever I need them.

1. Sleep Smarter

Sleep more, achieve more. That might be the most counterintuitive mantra you'll ever hear, but it's true. The body needs enough shut-eye each night to function properly and to recharge after a demanding day. Sleep also plays a critical role in immune function, metabolism, memory, learning, and other vital bodily functions. It's when the body does the majority of its repairing, healing, resting, and growing.

If you don't sleep enough, you're gradually wearing yourself, and your ability to meet daily challenges, down.

Sleeping Versus Sleeping Enough

But how much is enough? There is a big difference between the amount of sleep you can get by on and the amount you need to function optimally. Researchers at the University of California, San Francisco discovered that some people have a gene that enables them to do well on six hours of sleep a night. This gene, however, is very rare, appearing in less than 3 percent of the population. For the other 97 percent of us, six hours doesn't come close to cutting it. Just because you're able to function on five to six hours of sleep doesn't mean you wouldn't feel a lot better and get more done if you spent an extra hour or two in bed.

That may sound illogical. I can almost hear you thinking, *Spend more time in bed and get more done? How does that work?* But it has been well documented that enough sleep allows the body to function at higher levels of performance. You'll not only work better and faster, but your attitude will improve too.

The amount of rest each individual needs differs, but research shows that the average adult needs approximately seven to eight hours of sleep to restore the energy it takes to handle the demands of living each day. Children should rest longer than adults, newborns require up to 16 hours of slumber per day, and teens need between eight to nine hours of sleep.

The best way to figure out if you're meeting your sleep needs is to evaluate how you feel. If you're logging enough hours, you'll feel energetic and alert all day long, from the moment you wake up until your regular bedtime. If your sleep is inadequate, you'll reach for caffeine or sugar midmorning or midafternoon ... or both.

If you're like most people when you don't get enough rest, you have difficulty concentrating, thinking clearly, and remembering things. You might notice that you're ineffective or inefficient at home or work and blame these missteps on your busy schedule. The more sleep you miss, the more pronounced your symptoms become.

In addition, a lack of rest and relaxation can really do a number on your mood. Parenting is no place for crankiness! Don't discount the importance of sleep, even though it may be harder to get an uninterrupted night now that you have children. When you miss out on good nightly rest, your personality is affected, and generally you will be grumpier, less patient, and snap at people more easily. The result of missing out on critical, much-needed rest might make you a bear to be around, which is not much fun for anyone, yourself included.

When you get enough sleep, your body runs as it should, you're pleasant to be around, and your immune system is stronger. That's precisely when you'll make better choices with your kids and build a stronger family. Think of good sleep as the time when you turn on your inner light. Wake up rested and in a great mood because of your Life S.A.V.E.R.S., and you'll be able to meet the day's challenges with a positive attitude and respond with creativity.

The True Benefits of Sleep

You may not realize how powerful sleep actually is. While you sleep, your body undergoes processes that consolidate memories for better recall, help you recover from exercise and injuries, reduce stress, and improve your reaction time while driving.

2. Rest Your Mind

The conscious counterpart to sleep is *rest*. While some people use the terms interchangeably, they're really quite different. You might get eight hours of sleep, but if you spend all of your waking hours on the go, then you won't have any time to reflect or recharge your batteries. When you work all day, run from activity to activity with your kids after hours, and then finish with a quick dinner and a late bedtime, you don't allow for a period of rest.

Likewise, spending weekends taking the kids to soccer, volleyball, or basketball then heading out to see a football game, going to church, singing in the choir, attending several birthday parties, etc., can do more harm than good. While each of these activities is great, maintaining a fully packed schedule doesn't allow for time to rejuvenate.

What if, instead of being constantly on the go, you valued intentional quiet time, sacred space, and silence? How would that change your life, parenting abilities, and capability to achieve success in your family life?

It may seem counterintuitive to take time out when your to-do list is a mile long, but the fact is that more rest is a prerequisite to truly productive days.

Research proves that rest melts your stress away. Practices like yoga and meditation also lower your heart rate, blood pressure, and oxygen consumption. Slowing down and getting quiet means you can actually hear your own wisdom, inner knowledge, and inner voice to follow your parental intuition.

And yes, in case you're wondering, you'll be more productive, nicer to your friends and family members (not to mention your spouse or partner), and in general much happier as well. When we rest, it's like letting the earth lie fallow rather than constantly planting and harvesting. Our personal batteries need to be recharged. The best way is to do that is to truly and simply rest.

Easy Ways to Rest

Most of us confuse rest with recreation. To rest, we do things like hike, garden, work out, or even party. Any of these activities can be termed restful only because they are breaks from our everyday reality, but truthfully they are not, and cannot, be defined as rest.

Rest has been defined as a kind of waking sleep experienced while you are alert and aware. Rest is the essential bridge to sleep, and we achieve rest and sleep the same way: by making space for them and allowing them to happen. Every living organism needs rest, including you. When we don't take the time to rest, eventually its absence takes a toll on the body.

- If you take five minutes every morning during your Life S.A.V.E.R.S. to meditate or sit in silence, that is a great start.

- You can reserve one day a week for rest. Read, watch a movie, do something low-key with family, or even spend time alone. Try cooking at home, playing games with your kids, and enjoying each other's company.

- When you're driving, drive in silence: turn off the radio and stow your phone.

- Go for a walk without your earbuds in. Even a walk in nature without intention or goals, such as burning calories, can work.

- Turn off the television and other devices in favor of time for silence.

- Spend your time mindfully walking, writing, or soaking in a warm bath.

- Attend a retreat. It could be with your partner, a group of friends, your church, any community with which you are involved, or on your own.

Even taking a nap is a powerful way to rest and recharge. If I'm feeling drained during the day for some reason and still have many hours ahead, I won't hesitate to hit the reset button with a nap for 30–45 minutes.

It's helpful to set a specific time for rest. Put boundaries around it so you can claim that time.

The Rest Habit

Rest certainly isn't something we're taught in school, and it may not come naturally at first. You may find you need to learn it and make it a habit. Yoga Nidra and other restorative practices help you connect with yourself for deep relaxation.

Learning different contemplative practices and bringing them into your everyday life is an effective way to deeply rest your body, mind, and spirit. Think of how much you and your family will benefit from your taking the time to care for yourself.

3. Eat for Energy

A parent with low energy functions well below potential, and when it comes to energy, food may play the most critical role of all. If you're like most people, you make food choices based on taste first and consequences second (if you consider them at all). Yet, what makes us happy when we eat doesn't always give us maximum energy.

There is nothing wrong with eating foods that taste good, but if you want to be truly healthy and have the energy to be an effective parent, *you must learn to value the energy consequences of the food you eat above the taste.* Digesting food is one of the most energy-draining processes the body endures (think about how exhausted you feel after a big meal, like Thanksgiving dinner). Thus, eating living foods that contribute more energy to your body than they require to digest is the secret to maintaining extraordinary levels of energy *all day long.*

Bread, cooked meats, dairy products, and processed foods require a lot of energy to digest and contribute very little energy to your body, leaving you in an energy deficit. Foods like raw fruits, vegetables, nuts, and seeds typically give you more energy than they take, empowering you with an energy surplus to help you be at your best.

I've shifted my view of food from that of a reward, treat, or comfort to that of fuel. I want to eat delicious, healthy foods that boost my energy levels and allow me to keep going as long as I need to go.

Don't get me wrong. I still enjoy certain foods that are not the healthiest choices, but I strategically reserve them for times when I don't need to maintain optimum energy levels, such as in the evenings and on weekends.

The easiest way for me to start making better decisions about my eating was to pay attention to the way I felt after eating certain foods. I set a timer for 60 minutes after I finished each meal. When the timer went off, I assessed my energy levels. It didn't take long to recognize which foods gave me the biggest power boost and which ones didn't. I can clearly tell the difference in my energy level on the days when I eat sushi or a salad and the day I cave and eat a chicken sandwich or some pizza that smells so good. I find that incorporating as many of the right foods as I can often stops me from snacking on the unhealthy foods. Also packing my kids' lunches for them to take (or having them pack it themselves) and making sure to have healthy snacks available in the car prevents a lot of stops for the not-so-healthy stuff. It may take more effort, but the payoff is well worth that energy. Done properly, this is not only healthier, but it can be more cost effective than eating out.

The idea is to eat what you need to refuel and recharge your body and give yourself exactly what it takes to generate a sustained energy level. What would it be like to give your body what it needs to work and play for as long as you like? What would it be like to give yourself exactly what you truly deserve? Give yourself the gift of great health consciously chosen through what you eat and drink.

Eating throughout the day as an afterthought and stopping at a drive-through after you've hit the point of being famished might save you time and money in the short run, but the effects of low-quality food over time and the health issues it causes have been well documented. It is time to start building a new strategy.

Give some thought to the following:

- Can I start to consciously consider the health and energy consequences of what I eat and value that above the taste?

- Can I keep water with me at all times so that I can hydrate with intention and purpose and avoid becoming dehydrated?

- Can I plan my meals in advance, including snacks, so I can combat any patterns I have that don't serve me?

Yes, you can do all of these and much more. Think about how much better your life will be and how much more energy you will have for your family when you become conscious and intentional about your eating and drinking habits. Doing all of these at once is daunting. Try making one small change per month. Before you know it, you will have made massive transformations, one step at a time.

- You will spend more time consciously thinking about food (and truly enjoying the food you eat).

- You will spend less money on food.

- You will show your kids how to eat for health.

- You will get healthier and feel much better.

- Total bonus—you will settle at your natural weight effortlessly.

- Best bonus ever—you'll look and feel great!

Combining exercise, meditation, rest, and healthy food choices is a positive leap in the right direction for you on your path to becoming an exceptional parent and role model for your children.

I know what you're thinking, *This sounds great, but how do I get my kids to eat healthy foods too?* Nutrition expert Ellyn Satter's philosophy of child feeding allows children to explore food options within a structure you create. "The parent is responsible for *what, when,* and *where.* The child is responsible for *how much* and *whether* [they eat]." I have found this to be a helpful strategy. It makes it clear that our job as parents is to provide the structure and healthy options, and through them we empower our kids to make their own choices and trust them to follow their innate ability to regulate their food intake.

Another helpful tip is to have your kids be part of the process. Take them with you to the grocery store (or better yet, the farmers market) and have them help select the foods to prepare. Teach them about where their food comes from so they have a connection to it. Plant a backyard garden or try a potted vegetable or herb that you can use in cooking. You can easily grow spouts inside in just a few days; convenient kits can be ordered online. Take your children to visit a farm to see the animals and understand how vital agriculture is to our health. Have them help with meal preparation. Our son is my sous chef and takes great pride in chopping the veggies for dinner. And don't forget to have fun. For example, make purple smoothies—mix spinach with strawberries and blueberries—and have them for desert instead of ice cream. The more you involve your children in the process the more buy-in you will get on their end.

Don't forget hydration. As part of your Miracle Morning, you'll have had your first glass of water at the start of the day. I recommend including a full glass of water with each meal, which makes it easier to get the recommended eight to ten glasses a day. We intentionally refuel every three to four hours during the day. Our regular meals consist of some form of protein and vegetables. We snack frequently on fresh fruits and vegetables, nuts, and green smoothies. I try to plan our best meals for the days we need the most energy.

I believe that eating great most of the time, combined with exercise, gives us the latitude to eat what we want some of the time. I believe we can eat whatever we want, just not always as much as we'd like. I've learned to taste everything, but to eat just enough that I'm satisfied. It is not about depriving ourselves of the foods we love but eating in moderation and being present with our food. It's about appreciating the energy the food will give us and honoring where that food came from. When we consciously choose what we eat, it's really all about finding what works for you and is aligned with your body.

In the end, here is the simple thing to remember: food is fuel. It serves to get us from the beginning of the day all the way to the end, feeling great and having plenty of energy. Food can be used to your advantage to give you the endless energy you need to be the extraordinary parent you are meant to be.

Practice, Practice, Practice

Keep in mind that when you adopt these three practices—to sleep, rest, and eat better—you may at first feel uncomfortable. It can feel like when you're flying in a jetliner at 30,000 feet: upon descent, it almost always gets a little bumpy.

Your mind and body experience can be similar, and you may encounter some emotional turbulence. Many find it so uncomfortable that they flee by quickly becoming busy again. Resist the urge to run from the discomfort.

The more you integrate periods of rest and silence into your daily life, the bigger the payoff will be. During more tranquil periods, perhaps you won't need to rest as much, but periods of intensity (such as family reunions, holidays, or busy work days) may require more rest and silence than usual. It sounds counterintuitive, but the masterful meditator Mahatma Ghandi put it this way, "I have so much to accomplish today that I must meditate for two hours instead of one."

Final Thoughts on Energy Engineering

As a parent, you're in the trenches by default. You'll need to schedule rest, recharging, silence, and self-care in the same way you schedule the other appointments in your life. The energy you get back will reward you many times over.

So, remember what we discussed in this chapter to help you boost your energy levels and take better care of your health:

Step One: Make sleep a priority by choosing a consistent daily bedtime for both your kids and yourself. Decide on a consistent time when you will wake up to do your Miracle Morning and then back your way into a bedtime that ensures you get enough sleep. Maintain a specific bedtime for a few weeks (even on the weekends) to get your body into a rhythm. After a couple of weeks, feel free to play with the number of hours for sleep to optimize your energy levels. (Try bedtime sleep meditations if you struggle with falling asleep once you make it to bed.)

Step Two: Incorporate time into your daily calendar to rest and recharge. For example, Hal takes a two-hour lunch break every day, which gives him time to play basketball, something he loves to do and that re-energizes him. What can you plan in your day that will re-energize you? In addition to your Miracle Morning routine, schedule regular daily periods to rest and recharge. I schedule a massage every two weeks because that is something that recharges my energy supply.

Step Three: Plan longer periods of time for relaxation, such as a weekly date night, a quarterly overnight getaway, or an annual vacation. Many of us have cycles in our family and work calendars, and we should plan our relaxation around them. Schedule at least a few weeks of vacation throughout the year and once a quarter if you can manage it. Schedule it (and pay for it) ahead of time, so you will actually take it.

Step Four: Start eating for energy. Incorporate one new healthy meal into your diet each day. If you already have one healthy meal, add a second or include some new healthy snacks. Remember to keep water with you at all times so that you stay hydrated. I keep a bottle next to me in bed and one in the car too.

Advanced Step: Find ways to combine multiple practices. Plan a hike with friends or family or build a date night around preparing a healthy meal together.

Once you can create endless energy, what do you do with it? Unharnessed energy can be as detrimental as no energy at all. And that's why the next principle, Unwavering Focus, is just as important. I'll tell you about that in the next chapter.

PARENTING PROFILE
Rock Thomas

Rock is a successful entrepreneur and author as well as a sought-after inspirational speaker and motivational coach. His book is entitled, *The Power of Your Identity*.

Rock is the father of three children, a 24-year-old son and two daughters, ages 22 and 21.

Parenting Philosophy

Having come from a background where there wasn't much encouragement, I try to be the best cheerleader I can for my children. Wanting your dad to be proud of you, that never ends. Try to look at what your children are doing, applaud them, and acknowledge them. I think we live with four basic fears: We're not enough, we're not worthy, we're not important, and we can't do something. Telling somebody, "Well, you cut the carrots wrong," or "How come you don't have a better job?" or "You should step up and save more money," feeds those fears.

As a parent, your job is to keep your children safe. I try to do that with my children. I try to acknowledge them. Tell them I'm proud of them. Do things with them. Surprise them. Take my girls on date nights. I try to be that safe place for them and make them feel like they're doing great. They'll get their own hard lessons from life. I don't need to be correcting them.

What does your morning routine look like?

The morning ritual has been a secret weapon of mine for years. I was fortunate enough to be surrounded by successful people who were doing it. The very first thing for me is to shake off the cobwebs when I wake up, so I almost always get into moving my body. I'll often do a hundred push-ups, not in a row. In between sets, I'm filling my mind with new inspirational thoughts. I love to journal, so I write down things I'm grateful for, and I also feel the feelings of gratitude, and I think that's a mistake that some people make. You've got to emotionalize it. You have to feel the feelings consciously.

Are you an actor or are you a reactor?

In other words, do you have a plan for the role you're going to play in your life, or do you just react and play defense all the time? If you choose to have a morning ritual, you can be the actor you want throughout the day. If you do that, and your children see you do it, well, children will do more what you do than what you say.

Best Parenting Tips.

Teach your children how to learn. I was in interpersonal growth from a very young age, so I had my kids read books and learn how to speed type and different things like that. One great book I found is *Cheaper by the Dozen* by Frank Bunker Gilbreth, Jr. and Ernestine Gilbreth Carey. It's about a family with twelve kids, and how the father gets them to listen to recordings of new languages and stuff—while they're brushing their teeth. They were always in learning mode, and I tried to do the same things with my kids. If you can learn really well, you have an edge over other people, so learning to learn is very important.

Show respect to your kids' mother. I think respect and trust are two of the most important pillars in a relationship. So, hold each other in the highest esteem and do it in public. Always tell your children how great their mother is. There are things, obviously, that you may not appreciate so much, but it is really a matter of focusing on each other's good qualities. I think that made a difference as far as teaching respect.

Teach your children to respect other people. It's a very happy feeling when you're connected to another human being. The opposite of that is to judge them, disrespect them, and make them wrong. When you do this, it's really your own crap going on. So teach your kids that, even though you may value one thing and somebody else values something else, they can try to understand versus judge the other person.

Don't give advice unless they ask for it. If they come to me and say, "What about this? What about that?" I'll say, "You know, I'd love to give you my opinion. Would you like it?" I almost ask for permission to give them a piece of advice. Other than that, I try to say, "You're doing a great job."

Remember your kids are absorbing the messages you're sending. They say that, until you're seven years old, you're basically like a video camera, absorbing everything that's put in front of you. If you see your mother and father arguing all the time over money, you may develop a belief, because your brain is there to protect you, that money equals pain or hurt. Then when you grow up, you don't understand why every time you get some money, you give it away, lose it, gamble, or make a bad investment. But that's your brain telling you to repel money.

Teach them about money. Once a month, we get together and do what I call the Thomas Legacy. I teach them the seven levels of wealth mastery. I walk them through it, all the way from doing a budget to how to manage, how to save, how to simplify your life, and how to invest, etc., so that they have a really big picture, and they don't wait until they're forty years old with two kids, and they think, *Oh my God. I don't have any life insurance.*

Nurture connections between your kids. I was the youngest of six, and I felt so disconnected. I never tolerated that in my children. It's funny, people will say, "I've never seen children be so loving to each other." They're physically loving, and they never put each other down. They're in their twenties, but they're always supportive. The parent's job is to create that safe place for the children, and my children have created a safe place for each other too.

When they're older, hire them. Two of my kids work with me—and want to work with me. How great is it that I get to experience them in the working world, watch them grow, watch them contribute, hear from other people how great they're doing, and in my own little way contribute to their leadership skills when they ask for it? To me, that's a breakthrough for our family.

Final Word

As a parent, you can tell your kids, "There are parts of me that work really well. There are parts of me that don't. Take the best, and then make it better," and then your children can do the same thing, and that's pushing the human race forward. If we do that, then it becomes their obligation to take the baton and run a better race going forward. Also, the responsibility for you and me as parents doesn't end when our kids turn eighteen. It keeps on going. The work we continue to do on ourselves today pays a dividend for our children over a lifetime. I'm always trying to become a better person so that my children can live a happier, more fulfilled life.

PARENTING PROFILE
Marci Lock

Marci is known worldwide as the Ultimate Life Catalyst, mentoring global influencers, game changers, and high-producing leaders to help them live an epic life in all aspects. She transforms thousands of lives through her Average to Awesomeness Movement and Mind Body Breakthrough Programs, among others.

Marci is a single mom with two sons, ages 10 and 13.

Parenting Philosophy

You don't get what you deserve; you get what you're committed to. Results don't lie. We look at our results in life, and that's how we know what we're committed to. Because if you're dealing with a body that's overweight, and fat, and frustrated, and you have no energy, and you can't play with your kids, then that's what you're committed to. If you have the same kind of disconnect in your relationship, and you're not living with passion or purpose, or you're tolerating, settling, or sacrificing, then that's what you're committed to.

Best Parenting Tips

Ask how this can be fun? One question I always ask is, how can this be fun and easy? When we are in divine alignment, it feels good. If things don't feel good, they are probably out of alignment. The sun doesn't struggle to shine every day, birds don't struggle to fly, grass doesn't struggle to grow, and you don't struggle to breathe: we're effortlessly creating. As kids, we knew this, but then we got trained to disconnect from it. We unlearned the importance of fun and how it helps you figure out what you really want and what would make you feel good. So, one of the questions my kids and I always ask is, how can we make this fun and easy?

Reframe the question. Another question I like to ask is, what do you want to create? They might come complain to me about something, and I'll say, "I can hear that you're upset. What do you want to create? How can you create that so it is fun and easy?" We always want to bring ourselves back to feeling light and joy. If we're not in light and joy, then we know there's still something internally that gets to be cleared or looked at.

See your kids as teachers. I have these amazing growth partners, my two sons. As I started becoming more aware of when my kids would trigger me, and I'd recognize a way to turn it around and question: what's really going on inside me? I felt unheard, or I felt disrespected, and it all tied to the past. The little girl who never got to speak up or was shut down. These little things trigger us, and we become conscious of it, and that's when growth happens. When you question how you really relate to yourself and what's going on inside you, you start to improve your relationships. When I started to see my kids as my growth partners, and that we were on this journey together, parenting became such a different experience. It's evolved into authentic conscious conversations.

Keep a positive perspective. I remember sitting with my son one date night, and we were laughing and having a good time, and he said, "Mom, those people are staring at us. I think they're judging us." And I said, "That's an interesting thought. What if your thought was that they are watching you, and they're thinking you're so happy, and they wished they could be this happy?" We talked about changing perception, showing up, and how we create our own happy.

Have regular date nights with your kids. Another way that we create a lot of fun is we have regular date nights. I have a date night each week with each of my sons, and I even have a date night with myself. That has been evolutionary for our connection, and our relationship. Just giving quality time for fun, play, and what they want to do.

Do it now. I remember reaching a point where I said, if I want an amazing relationship with my kid, I've got to do something different. I don't want to be one of those entrepreneurs that says someday when the business is built, someday when the money is there, someday we'll take vacations, someday we'll play. The time to connect with your kids is now. I started by picking one day a week at 3:00 when they're done with school to reserve a two-hour time block of play. Then I started to change that to a couple times a week, and soon it became 3:00 every day. We built on that and created the lifestyle that you get when you believe you're worthy and deserving of it. You create the balance for yourself.

You can create the life you want. My friend says, "Show me your schedule, and I'll show you your priorities." I think that's powerful. This is why I believe everything in your life gets to be awesome and amazing. Tell yourself, "I'm worthy of awesome relationships. How do I get to create that? What else do I get to let go of? How do I get to honor myself or become more worthy?" Create a life that you want. Give yourself permission to live the life you love and create that same kind of life with your kids.

Parenting Success Story

I teach my kids to see how they can make people happy. We created things like our "Columbia bag" (because I started doing it when we went to Columbia) where we'd throw in lots of different toys and money for homeless people. Whenever we go in a restaurant or a store, we grab our bag, and we find little kids to give toys or stickers to or homeless people to give money, treats, or food. They ask, "What are you doing?" And we say, "We want to give you a gift," and they're so surprised. It shows how closed off the world is to that kind of interaction. These are just ways to shift the negative things that may have happened in school during the day. We get to turn it around, and then they get to focus on a new behavior. It's priceless for sure.

Final Word

Nineteen out of twenty people fail at getting what they want, and there's a big reason why. They don't allow themselves to see what's actually possible. It's beautiful for people to see that their lives can be amazing. The Miracle Morning shows you what you can have with your family when you start to shift the way that you do things. It offers a different learning system and creates a new model for people. I'm happy to be a part of it.

— 6 —
NOT-SO-OBVIOUS PARENTING PRINCIPLE #3:
UNWAVERING FOCUS

It is not enough to be industrious; so are the ants. What are you industrious about?
— Henry David Thoreau, American author, naturalist, and transcendentalist

We've all met that person. You know—*that* person. The one who runs marathons, coaches little league, volunteers for her son's school lunch program, cooks great meals, and maybe writes a memoir on the side. And on top of all that? She's an incredible mother, head of the PTA, winning awards at every year-end meeting, and knocking it out of the park when it comes to everything involving her family life.

I bet you know someone like that—someone who seems amazingly productive. What you might not realize, though, is exactly how she does it. Maybe you always thought she was lucky. Or gifted. Or connected. Or had the right personality. Or was born with superpowers!

While those things can help when it comes to parenting, I know from experience that the real superpower behind every unbelievably productive mom or dad is *focus*.

Focus is the ability to maintain clarity about your highest priorities, take all the energy you've learned to generate for yourself, channel it into what matters most, and keep it there, regardless of what is going on around you or how you feel. This ability is key to becoming an exceptional parent.

When you harness the power of focus, you don't become superhuman, but you can achieve seemingly superhuman results. And the reasons for this are surprisingly straightforward.

- **Focus makes you more effective.** Being effective doesn't mean doing the most things or doing things the fastest. It means doing the *right* things. You engage in the activities that create forward momentum toward your life's goals.

- **Focus makes you more efficient.** Being efficient means doing things with the fewest resources, such as time, energy, or money. Every time your mind wanders away from your family goals, you waste those things—particularly time. In parenting, time is always in demand, so every moment that your focus wavers is another moment lost.

- **Focus makes you productive**. When you focus on your highest priorities, do the right things, and do them in the right way, you get more done with less effort. Too often we confuse being busy—engaged in activities that don't produce results—like alphabetizing your DVD collection or picking up after your kids when they are capable of doing it themselves—with being productive. By taking the steps that we're about to cover, you'll learn how to develop the habit of unwavering focus and join the ranks of the most productive parents in the world.

If you combine those benefits, you will achieve *a lot* more. Perhaps the greatest value of focus, however, is that rather than scattering your energy across multiple areas of your life and getting mediocre results across the board, you will release untapped potential *and* improve your life.

Now let's turn your Miracle Morning to the task. Here are the three steps you need to turn your morning time into focused, productive time.

Step One: Find Your Best Environment(s) to Focus

Let's start here: *You need an environment that supports your commitment to unwavering focus.* It might be your spare bedroom, or it could be your backyard. No matter how modest, though, you need a place where you go to focus.

Part of the reason for this is simple logistics. If your materials are scattered from the trunk of your car to the kitchen counter, you can't be effective. A bigger reason, however, is that **having a place where you focus triggers the habit of focusing**. Sit at the same desk to do great work at the same time every day, and soon enough you'll find yourself slipping into the zone just by sitting down in that chair.

We have a room in our home that is dedicated to the Miracle Morning practice. It is our sanctuary, and we find we are drawn to this room in the morning to complete our Miracle Morning practice. We each have chairs we love for meditation, and before we go to bed at night we place our journals, books, and other resources where they are easily accessible. This space also serves as a place to stop in and meditate even if it's just for a few minutes, to get clarity around what's important again. You do not have to have a whole room for this either. A dedicated chair in the corner of your living room works just as well.

Step Two: Clear the Clutter

Stuff is a focus killer, and it's our next stop on this journey. I know what you're thinking. Kids create clutter, and there's nothing you can do about it. Not true! First of all, there are two kinds of clutter, mental and physical, and we all have them both. We carry around thoughts in our minds, like these: *My sister's birthday is coming up. I have to get her a gift and card. I had a great time at dinner the other night. I need to send the host a thank-you note. I have to answer the email from my new client before I leave the office today.*

And we accumulate physical items: Unused toys, broken things, stacks of paper, old magazines, sticky notes, clothes we never wear, the pile of junk in the garage, trinkets, knickknacks, and tokens.

Clutter of either type creates the equivalent of a heavy fog, and to become focused, you need to be able to *see*. To clear your vision, you'll want to get those mental items out of your head and collected so you can relieve the mental stress of trying to remember them. And then, you'll want to get those physical items out of your way.

Here's a simple process to help you clear the fog and create the clarity you need to focus.

- **Create a master to-do list.** You probably have lots of things that haven't been written down yet—start with those. And all those sticky notes that clutter your desk, computer screen, planner, countertops, refrigerator ... Are there other places? Put those notes and action items on your master list. Put them all in one central location, whether that's a physical journal or a list on your phone, so that you can clear your mental storage. Feeling better? Keep going; we're just getting started.

- **Purge your workspace.** Schedule a half (or full) day to go through every stack of paper, file folder stuffed with documents, and tray full of unopened mail ... You get the gist. Throw out or shred what you don't need. Scan or file the ones that matter. Note in your journal any items that need your attention and cannot be delegated then pick a time in your schedule to complete them.

- **Declutter your life.** Wherever possible, clean up and clear out every drawer, closet, cabinet, and trunk that doesn't give you a sense of calm and peace when you see it. This includes your car. This might take a few hours or a few days. Schedule a short time each day until everything is complete. Saying, "I just need a weekend to declutter," is a sure way to never start. Pick a single drawer and start there. You'll be surprised at how the little bursts of work accumulate. We spend about 15–20 minutes every evening as a family putting stuff back in its place. Getting the kids involved teaches them responsibility and will provide more hands to get the work done quickly. The more fun you can make it the better! Try S.J. Scott and Barrie Davenport's book, *10-Minute Declutter: The Stress-Free Habit for Simplifying Your Home* for suggestions.

Getting physically and mentally organized will allow you to focus at a level you would never believe possible—and it's better for your kids as well. It leaves your energy nowhere to go except to what *matters*.

Step Three: Build Unwavering Focus

Once you identify your focus place and begin the process of de-cluttering your life, you should experience a remarkable increase in focus simply from clearing the fog in your mind.

Now, it's time to take things to the next level. I use three questions to improve my focus.

- What's working that I should *keep doing* (or do more of)?
- What do I need to *start doing* to accelerate results?
- What do I need to *stop doing* immediately that's holding me back from going to the next level?

If you can answer those three questions and take action on the results, you'll discover a whole new level of productivity you probably didn't think was possible. Let's look at each question in detail.

What Do You Need to Keep Doing (or Do More of)?

Let's face it, not all parenting tactics and strategies are created equal. Some work better than others. Some work for a while and then become less effective. Some even make things worse.

Right now, you're probably doing a lot of the right activities, and you'll be nodding right along as you read the coming chapters on three P's of parenting. If you already know the things you're doing that are working, jot those down. Perhaps you're constantly looking for educational activities for your kids, for example. Put that on the "what's working" list. Perhaps a parenting group is delivering great tips—add that to the list, too.

Make sure you're choosing things that actually contribute to increasing your parenting success. It's easy to keep the things you *like* doing, but you need to make sure that the activities you're doing are directly related to raising strong, healthy kids; strengthening your parenting community and your family; and increasing the good times you all have together. For example, many parents believe that giving their kids a time-out is a good way to discipline, but research shows how ineffective this tactic is in changing behavior in the long run. A much more effective tool is a "time in," where the parent will sit with the child to help them calm down and then redirect them.

At the end of this chapter, you'll have an opportunity to capture in your journal the activities that are working. (Among them, I hope, will be that you've started doing the Life S.A.V.E.R.S.) Everything that's on that list is a *keep doing* until it's replaced by something even more effective.

For all of the "keep doing" activities on your list, make sure you're completely honest with yourself about *what you need to be doing more of* (in other words, what you're currently not doing enough of). If it's something you think you should be doing, such as keeping the art supplies organized or the underwear folded, but it's not moving you forward toward your important parenting goals, it doesn't belong on your list. Perfection is not one of the goals here. Overworking yourself is ultimately unproductive and takes your focus off the important things.

Keep doing what's working, and depending on how much more you want to achieve, simply do *more* of what's working.

What Do You Need to Start Doing?

Once you've captured what's working and determined what you need to do more of, it's time to decide what else you can do to accelerate your success.

I have a few top-shelf parenting suggestions to prime the pump and get you started.

- Pack lunches and school bags the night before (if the kids are old enough, have them do this step)
- Plan date night
- Conduct weekly family meetings
- Schedule quarterly family board meetings (one-on-one time with one parent and child)
- Perform cleanup time every day
- Cook together
- Volunteer at your children's school or together for a local charity
- Give the kids age-appropriate responsibilities

- Make family dinner a priority, put electronics away, and ask great questions
- Plan a weekly menu and shop for the items together
- Plan family game nights

I caution you to not become overwhelmed here. Keep in mind that Rome wasn't built in a day. You don't need to identify 58 action items and implement them by tomorrow. The great thing about having a daily scribing practice as part of your Miracle Morning means you can capture everything. Then, one or two at a time, add them to your success toolbox until they become habits. Incremental improvements have a magical way of accumulating.

What Do You Need to Stop Doing?

By now you've most likely added a few items to start doing. If you're wondering where the time is going to come from, this might be your favorite step of all. It's time to let go of the things you've been doing that don't serve you and your family to make room for the ones that do.

I'm fairly sure you do a number of daily activities you will be relieved to stop doing, thankful to delegate to someone else or grateful to release.

Why not stop

- eating unhealthy, energy-draining foods that suck the life and motivation out of you?
- doing unnecessary household chores?
- replying to texts and emails instantly?
- answering the phone? (Let it go to voicemail and reply when the timing works best for you.)
- reading and posting on social media sites?
- watching hours of television a day?
- beating yourself up or worrying about what you can't change?
- yelling at the children?

Or, if you want to improve your focus dramtically in one simple step, try this easy fix: *Stop responding to buzzes and sounds like a trained seal.*

Do you really need to be alerted when you receive texts, emails, and social media notifications? Nope, didn't think so. Go into the settings of your phone, tablet, and computer and turn all your notifications OFF.

Technology exists for your benefit, and you can take control of it this very minute. How often you check your phone messages, texts, and email can and should be decided by *you*. Let's face it, most of us do not have jobs that will result in a life-or-death situation if we do not respond immediately to a call, text, or email. We don't need to be accessible 24/7/365 except to our children. An effective alternative is to schedule times during the day to check on what's happening, what needs your immediate attention, what items can be added to your schedule or master to-do list and what can be deleted, ignored, or forgotten. As a stay-at-home mom, I have a babysitter come a few hours a week to play with the kids so I can focus on my master to-do list. If your kids go to school or still nap, you can use some of that time to focus on your list.

Final Thoughts on Unwavering Focus

Most parents would be shocked to discover just how little time they spend on important activities relevant to real growth each day. As parents, our time can easily be taken up by small tasks that seem important in the moment but are a waste of time we don't have. Today, or in the next 24 hours, schedule 60 minutes to focus on the single most important task you do, and you'll be amazed not only by your productivity, but also by how empowering it feels.

Focus is like a muscle that you build over time. And, like a muscle, you need to show up and do the work to make it grow. Cut yourself some slack if you falter, but keep pushing forward. It will get easier. It might take you time to learn to focus, but every day that you try, you'll continue to get better at it. Ultimately, this is about *becoming* someone who focuses, which starts with seeing yourself as such. I recommend that you add a few lines to your affirmations about your commitment to unwavering focus and what you will do each day to develop it.

Remember the steps we discussed in this chapter on the importance of unwavering focus and the ways to increase it in your life.

Step One: Free your mind with a brain dump. Unload all those little to-do lists floating around in your head. Create a master to-do list in your journal (which could be your Life S.A.V.E.R.S. journal).

Step Two: Build your Three Unwavering Focus lists:

- What I need to keep doing (or do more of)
- What I need to start doing
- What I need to stop doing

Step Three: For the next week, keep a list of all the things you spend time doing and how long you spend on each task or activity. What can be automated, outsourced, or delegated? How much time did you spend on truly productive, important activities? Repeat this process until you are clear on what your process is, and start time blocking your days so that you're spending close to 80 percent of your time on tasks that bring harmony and joy to your life. Delegate the rest.

By now, you've added some pretty incredible action items and focus areas to your parenting toolbox. In the next section, I'll help you strengthen your parenting skills and combine them with the Life S.A.V.E.R.S. in ways you might not have imagined before!

PARENTING PROFILE

Seth Campbell

Seth is Chairman of the Board and a founding member at Five Doors Real Estate Team in Baltimore, Maryland. He is also a Regional Director for Keller Williams Realty in the Maryland/ DC region.

He has a 14-year-old son from a previous relationship and three children with his wife—a 6-year-old son, a 4-year-old daughter, and an infant son.

Parenting Philosophy

There are two paths you can go down with anything. The "No, Why" path and the "Yes, How" path. We are "Yes, How" people. Here's an example. My son sees a toy that he wants in a store and starts with the typical four-year-old meltdown. I ask a question like, "How would you like to be able to buy that?" His mindset immediately switches to problem solving. "Yes, I can buy this for myself. Here's how I would do it. I put it up on the goal chart. Then I would start working towards it at 70 percent of my money." My wife and I use this technique in parenting. If our child says "I want to stay up late and do this." We say, "Yes, you can do that. Here's how." It would have to be on a Friday night when he's done certain things.

What do you do to shift your mindset from CEO leader to father?

I'm very purposeful about that. It's through a schedule, and it's through priorities. I have five-year goals. I have one-year goals. I have experimented with my own family to figure out what matters most to them, what has the biggest impact. Then I calendar it and do it. I time block for these things to prevent me from getting out of balance and putting the business too far in front. For example, I used to have kid time when I got home from work. But I found that I wasn't the best version of myself. I was tired and exhausted from the workday. So I changed it to mornings. Every morning before I go to work, I interact one-on-one with each of my kids.

Best Parenting Tips

Take time to communicate. When each child was born, I gave them their own email address. I send email, pictures, or videos of them doing something funny. I gave them access to my Evernote journal so that when they get older, they will have this whole history that they can look through.

Pour out your cup each day. I want to be the kind of father who pours his cup out every day so that I can come back for a refill. I don't want the water to get stagnant. I don't want to hold on to it for myself. I get real clear on what today's lesson is, and I pour it all out to the kids and at work that same day so when my head hits the pillow I know I gave it all.

Teach your kids about money. If you ask them about money, my kids will say, "It's a tool. It's like a hammer. It could be used to hurt somebody, or it could be used to build something. Save somebody from being homeless." I use the 70-30 rule that we get from Gary Keller and others. Seventy percent of their money goes towards spending. Ten percent goes towards saving. Ten percent goes towards investing and ten percent towards giving. They have four different envelopes that they use every time they earn money.

Don't underestimate your kids' abilities. It's incredible what children can understand at a young age. It's way more than what Dora the Explorer teaches them. That's probably a reflection of how we all underestimate ourselves, right? We all have greater abilities than we think we do. It's important to be aware of when we start to project that onto our children if we're not careful about it.

Put away your own electronics. I caught myself at night when the kids run up to me with this device, my cellphone, physically in my hand—actually positioned between us, like a mini wall. What message am I sending to my daughter when she's looking at me and

I'm looking at the device in between us? Be prepared to fully drop everything, be present, look in their eyes, and really listen.

Use systems. I'll share a quick system. I had my kids write out on 12 different index cards what they would love to do with daddy. They put them in a box, and the first Saturday of every month, they draw a card randomly. When we go on our individual date that month we do the activity on the index card.

Relationship with the Creator. The beginning of leadership is your ability to lead yourself first, right? We believe that that comes from our first relationship with our creator. That is what gives us the wisdom to lead ourselves in the most effective way. None of our other relationships in the world will ever surpass how well we do in our first relationship.

Adjust your perspective. I adjust my perspective all the time. Any time I start to feel myself getting stressed out, I say, "You know what? I'm at a ground level perspective, really close to the ground. What would it look like if I raised and widened my perspective? If I went up to the five thousand-foot view and saw it in context with everything else that's going on, not just this meltdown that's happening right now? What if I widened it to this week or this month or this year? This is just one little blip that we're going through."

Set goals. We like the idea of setting big, lofty goals and every day incrementally working towards them. Every day, let's take a step closer and recognize that that's the way we win in life, having that perspective.

Don't hesitate to play. My kids have taught me the importance of fun. Something happened when I went into these golden years; I became a lot less fun and a lot more serious about life. They've taught me to let it go, have fun, laugh like kids do. It's helped me to be calmer, happier, and more relaxed and to enjoy and be in the moment.

Final Word

Failure is a perspective thing. Maybe something feels like a failure right now, but in a year's time, it was just a learning curve. We're all scared of failing as parents—particularly given what we believe is on the line here. My advice is let that go. Make mistakes. Do it. Get out there and find out what makes the biggest impact on your kids, what makes them light up. I think as parents we've got to let all this stress of being a good parent go. Just drop all that and fail forward.

PARENTING PROFILE

Cheryl Lowery

Cheryl is a stay-at-home mother of two boys, Connor, age six and Colton, who is three, who lives near Philladelphia. Her husband, Shawn, is a real estate entrepreneur. Her older son, Connor, is on the autism spectrum.

How has practicing the Miracle Morning changed you as a parent?

I honestly was not gifted with patience. Resourcefulness and re-silience, yes, but patience ... not so much. Meditation, silence, and affirmations can lead to patience. So can reading. I recently read *The Reason I Jump* by Naoki Higashida, who is mostly a nonverbal 13-year-old boy with autism. It reminded me to be more patient with my son because there are simply times when he just can't help it; he's wired differently. I would not have read it unless I was making the time to do so during my Miracle Mornings. Days after reading it, Connor had a tantrum that involved throwing an art project that was full of wet paint. It covered the walls, floors, dining room table, and buffet table with a dark aqua-colored paint. I was able to hold myself together. I didn't yell. I simply sent Connor and his brother to play a game with Connor's home aide while I spent the next 30 minutes cleaning off the various surfaces the paint had covered. At that moment, I was a good parent practicing patience, which I may not have been able to do before.

How have you become purposeful in your parenting?

I have become more purposeful in my parenting by introducing the Miracle Morning to my children. We started with affirmations and paying compliments to each other. We are able to work on areas of need by including them in our affirmations. In this way, we can put a positive spin on it. For example, one of Colton's affirmations is "I like to try new foods." As you can guess, he didn't like to try new foods before this, but the more we introduced the idea, the more willing he became, and sometimes he even liked them. Another one of Colton's affirmations is "I use a nice voice." Connor, on the other hand, eats pretty much everything but has difficulties with rigidity. One of his affirmations is "I am flexible and play nice." Both boys have some of the same affirmations, such as, "I am a good listener" and "I make good choices."

How do you stay playful as a parent?

This is surprisingly difficult for me. Growing up, I was always naturally good with kids, consistently at the top of babysitting lists and winning awards for being the favorite camp counselor. I assumed I would automatically become a great parent. But, once I had my own kids and experienced that kind of exhaustion (lessened now by my Miracle Mornings), I noticed I wasn't playing with them as much as I felt I could or should. I've been working on that. I've always brought them to playgrounds daily, pushed them on swings, let them throw rocks in the water, traveled to zoos or museums, taken them to music, gymnastics, or swim lessons, and have really enjoyed *watching* them— not my phone.

If I weren't paying attention to them, I would miss little, yet huge moments like Connor taking my hand to lead me somewhere to ask for more water. For him, as a six-year-old, it was a major milestone, one that his little brother had done countless times at age two or three. But thankfully, I was present and paying attention.

Shawn does a great job playing Frisbee, soccer, basketball, baseball, or bowling with the boys. He goes down the slide with them and plays with them on the playground. He plays at Chuck E. Cheese's or mini golfs with them on Daddy date nights (each week one of them gets a turn to pick where he will go with Daddy that evening).

What perspective(s) do you think are important in being the best parent you can be?

Thankfulness. Appreciation. Gratitude. Although having autism is difficult for the individual and those around him, it does not affect his overall health. Connor is not sick. He does not have a shorter life expectancy. We have no serious health issues. My child may have struggles, but he does not have cancer or any life-threatening illness. His diagnosis, while part of him, does not define him. He has strengths and weaknesses like anyone else. The diagnosis is simply a means to access the services to address those weaknesses. We want what any parent wants, for our children to be happy. We hope to leave a legacy for them that would make them proud.

What resources would you share with other parents?

We use a social worker at a developmental pediatrics practice to gather ideas for services in our area, and we ask her opinion on what is good and bad. As a science and research based family, we try to get articles from reliable sources such as the National Institutes of Health. This article from NIH has been particularly helpful: "Complementary and Alternative Medicine Treatments for Children with Autism Spectrum Disorders" by Susan E Levy M.D.

We do not recommend random Internet searches for information.

For books and other resources, we like the following:

- *Fill a Bucket: A Guide to Daily Happiness for Young Children* by Carol McCloud, Katherine Martin, and David Messing

- *Oh, the Places You'll Go!* by Dr. Seuss

- *Pete the Cat and his Magic Sunglasses* by Kimberly & James Dean (or any other Pete the Cat book)

- *The Verbal Behavior Approach: How to Teach Children with Autism and Related Disorders* by Mary Lynch Barbera

- *Uniquely Human: A Different Way of Seeing Autism* by Barry M. Prizant, PhD

- *Life, Animated: A Story of Sidekicks, Heroes, and Autism* by Ron Suskind

- This is a great article on autism—I cry every time I read it: http://momastery.com/blog/2014/07/21/letter-about-autism/

- This podcast episode hits home for me as the parent of a child on the autism spectrum: http://www.radiolab.org/story/juicervose/

Has doing the Miracle Morning with Connor helped him in other areas of his life?

Yes. Any time we can highlight Connor's strengths, I find it to be a win-win scenario. We want to build him up, yet we work for countless hours each week on his deficiencies. That's a tough life for a four- to six-year-old. He has become more creative in his play recently. Among his areas of strength are his diet and his gross motor skills, so I feel he has a good handle on his physical health. The affirmations increase his awareness of his positive qualities. He loves to read and has become quite good at it. Meditation is an area I would love to concentrate on with him in the future as I can see only positive benefits for him becoming more mindful and present.

Parenting Success Story

By using *Teach Your Child to Read in 100 Easy Lessons* by Siegfried Engelmann (The Proven SRA DISTAR Reading Program Adapted for Parent and Child), I was able to advance Connor to a second-grade reading level before he entered kindergarten. This is huge for a couple reasons. First, the child who has difficulty with language is able to read; that's pretty cool. Second, task demands are one of Connor's triggers, something that can set off a tantrum. Now that the school doesn't have to teach him how to read, that is one less set of demands that they need to place on him, and they can focus on other areas of need, such as social skills.

After sending a five-page (single spaced) email *advocating* for a one-on-one aide for my son when he was in kindergarten, I received the following response within 48 hours:

"We have discussed your concerns and will include a summary statement of your concerns in Connor's IEP. In addition, [his teacher] will modify the adult support in Connor's IEP to include a PCA (1:1) for Connor during the Regular Education/Kindergarten portion of his day." Total parenting win and a good definition of the word *advocate*.

Best Parenting Tips

Surround yourself with knowledgeable people. Finding a respected and knowledgeable pediatrician or family practitioner who is willing to take the time to help is key. In addition, I am lucky my sister is a pediatrician. Her specialty is infectious disease, not child development, but she's still a pediatrician! I have friends who also help. One has a son with special needs (Prader-Willi Syndrome) and is also a behavioral specialist (BSC). Another friend is a special education teacher in elementary education and is the mom of triplets. One friend attended an individualized education program meeting with me.

Get a helpful team. It takes a village to raise a neurotypical child, but it takes a team for a child on the spectrum or with similar developmental delays. The home and school staff, aides, therapists, and behavioral specialists that we have worked with have been so patient and have helped us provide Connor with an upward trajectory. Our first (wraparound) team was integral in increasing Connor's communication. Our current team has been vastly helpful in the areas of play, increasing flexibility, decreasing rigidity, and improving social skills.

Don't reinvent the wheel. Of course every child is different, but learn from those who've gone before you. We have been apt to follow any advice that our developmental pediatrician provides us. That included Susan Chaplick's preschool program, a privately-paid early intervention program at Bryn Mawr College, which has been such a giant portion of Connor's impressive gains.

Take advantage of online resources. Autism Speaks has a wonderful "First 100 Days Kit" for those first three months or so after your child receives a diagnosis. Lots of online resources, including special needs parents groups for your area on Facebook that can be helpful and might lead you to find some of your better friends on the journey and in life.

Final Word

While autism is just one facet of the special needs community, we identify with the special needs struggles as a family. Parenting a special needs child is just different. It is not better. It is not worse. I am not better. I am not worse. It's just different. I need to remind myself to practice patience more. When I do, I can better appreciate those times when the hard work pays off and success becomes ours to cherish. As an austism parent, you are constantly trying to pull your child into "our" world while desperately attempting to understand his world at the same time. To quote one of our favorite books, *Oh, the Places You'll Go!* by Dr. Seuss, "Life's a Great Balancing Act." That has truly become our family motto.

— 7 —
EXCEPTIONAL PARENTING SKILL #1:
Purposeful Parenting

*As parents, we guide by our unspoken example. It is only when
we're talking to them that our kids aren't listening.*
—Robert Brault, Author of *Round up the Usual Subjects:
Thoughts on Just about Everything*

When you apply your Miracle Morning practice to parenting, something wonderful happens: You'll find yourself setting intentions and focusing your efforts on becoming a truly exceptional parent. Parents who are purposeful are able to lead their families more effectively. You'd be surprised how many well-meaning parents get this wrong—they let their kids set the day's agenda. In contrast, purposeful parents direct events rather than letting events direct them. This doesn't mean that they're in total control; no one who has actually been a parent would expect to be. But purposeful parents take the initiative and set the tone for the day—starting with their Miracle Morning.

Purposeful parents stay informed and use all the resources available to improve their parenting. They value connectedness with their children and formulate strategies to protect it. They value clear communication with their children and with each other. And they know the value of creating and maintaining partnerships with other parents, teachers, caregivers, doctors (and other experts), with each other, and with their children. I'll be taking each of these ideas and exploring it in greater detail later in this chapter. But first, to become purposeful, it's essential to have a vision of what your ideal family life would look like.

Creating a Purposeful Vision

Your vision of the ideal family life may look drastically different from mine. Every family is different. Your ideal family life will reflect your values, goals and priorities, and the plan to move intentionally toward those goals is highly customizable. You may be thinking, *It's great that you are following your vision, but how do I discover and form my own vision?* It's easier than you might think! When you follow the four-step visioning process below, it will help you to create a clear picture of your ideal life and identify the action steps that will turn your vision into reality.

Feel free to take some time to complete this process. If it seems overwhelming at first, take it one step at a time. The point is to ask the important questions, find the answers, and become purposeful about moving your life in the right direction. I agree with Bill Gates, "Most people overestimate what they can do in one year and underestimate what they can do in ten years." So think BIG, be purposeful, and reverse engineer.

Four Steps to Create Your Ideal Family Life

Step One: Develop a vision

Step one is designed to get you thinking about the kind of family life would create the most fulfillment. You can start by getting out your journal and asking yourself some thought-provoking questions. What would your ideal family life look like? What gives you energy and makes your heart sing? If fear were not holding you back, what would you do with your time? Where do you see your family in five years? Your vibe attracts your tribe, so who do you surround yourself with? Where are you living and what environment have you created in your home? What are you doing to make a difference in the world?

Take a trip to the future. Start the vision by selecting a date three to five years in the future. Close your eyes and imagine your life in vivid detail just as you want it to be. Once you can see, feel and hear your future, with as much detail as possible, write out your vision, as if you're living it right now. From the perspective of your future self, describe the person you have become and the things have you have done to create your ideal life. When writing down my vision, I start with these words, "The date is _____, and my life is awesome because ..." I finish it with, "either this or something better."

As you go through these questions, take the time to write out your answers. This process can be part of your daily Scribing and Visualization practices. You also have the option to create time specifically to focus on diving deep on this visioning process. For access to a helpful guided meditation to take you 5 years into the future, check out Jenai Lane's free online course. http://www.spiritcoachtraining.com/freecourse/

It's also important to understand your desires, what motivates you, and what really lies beneath your answers to these questions. I recommend asking deeper questions about your vision. What specifically does it look like? Do you want your family to travel together? Is a family dinner every night possible? If not, maybe a family breakfast? Is a family meeting something that would help your communication? Why is having this vision important to you? What will having it do for you? How will you feel when you are living the life of your dreams?

When you write, try to be comprehensive and focus on what matters to you. It's designed to get you thinking about what a healthy, successful, and playful family looks like. There's no limit to the questions you can ask. The important thing is to create a vision that is inspiring and allows you to do more of what you enjoy as a family.

Another thing I have found helpful in the visioning process is to create a vision board either individually or as a family (or both). Every year, we make a large vision board together to help remind us of what is important that year. It is not only a great family activity, but it truly primes the subconscious mind to attract that vision. The reason vision boards are so powerful (and affirmations and visualization for that matter) is related to the way our brains are wired.

We each have a loose network of neurons in our brains called the reticular activating system (RAS). The RAS filters information so your senses do not become overloaded and helps bring relevant information to your attention. For example, you might be driving on the highway and pass several speed limit signs but not notice them at all. When you pass a police officer and want to make sure you are driving the speed limit, you notice them every mile. This is your RAS at work. Advertisers keenly play to this system in their marketing. So, what if you created the perfect advertisement for the family life you want and consciously programmed your mind through your RAS to help attract it? That is exactly what a vision board is, an advertisement for your ideal family life!

Creating a vision board is simple, and the great news is that there is no wrong way to do it. Personally, I like to start with big images. Landscapes of beautiful places where I'd like to travel work really well for this first step. Then I fill it up with smaller images that speak to me. If you lack clarity of vision, it can be fun to let the universe select your images. Clear your mind with a meditation then let a page number come to mind. Turn to that page and cut out whatever speaks to you to include on your board. It's okay to include material things on a vision board, but I'd advise you to let this be more about who you want to become and the experiences you want to have as a family than what you want to own. The things we own can sometimes start to own us, and you can't take them with you in the end anyway. Try to tap into the emotions or the symbolism behind the images more than the literal interpretation of them. At the end of step one, you should have a clear picture of your ideal family life.

Step Two: Define what you need to do to start moving in that direction

Once you start seeking answers, they tend to appear. In fact, you might find that you can generate several ways to achieve your family goals once you know what they are. Break your vision down into parts if you need to and then formulate a written action plan for how you're going to guide your family in that direction. Maybe you think that a successful family spends two hours of quality time together every day, but your kids spend all their free time on computers. What's your plan to move them toward less computer time? Would going cold turkey work? Or maybe a more gradual approach would be better? That depends on the family. The point here is to think about the direction you want to move and then create a plan to make that change.

For this step, you may find that gathering information from many sources helps. Take advantage of your family network. Ask other parents, teachers, doctors, or relatives for their advice and recommendations. You can read books and use the Internet as a resource as well.

Step Three: Track your progress

Changing a family culture can be like changing the direction of a cargo ship: it happens slowly and by degrees. It's best to track your progress and celebrate small successes. Try things more than once. What doesn't work one day might very well work on another day. Remember that families are made up of people, and people have good days and bad days. Make a note of what works and what doesn't. And don't forget to be patient.

You can incorporate your plan into your daily affirmations and visualizations to help you stay motivated and engaged. Remember, you are working toward the ideal family situation you envisioned in step one. The goal is well worth all the effort!

Step Four: Constantly update and evolve your approach

As you continue to put into place the steps to achieve your ideal family life, don't be afraid to modify your approach when you find things that aren't working. We used the example of the family breakfast in step one. This is a creative alternative to getting the togetherness behind the idea of the family dinner. If dinners aren't possible, breakfast could be a good substitute.

Purposeful Vision in Action

I'm going to share a story of how we got purposeful as a family to illustrate the process. Mike and I love to travel. When we first had children, we vowed that we would find a way to continue to travel as a family. We actually hiked Mount Kilimanjaro when I was four months pregnant (we got my doctor's okay first) because we had already paid for the once in a lifetime trip and didn't want to miss it!

After Tyler was born, we stayed mostly in the country. But like his parents, our son was a great traveler, even as an infant! He went on his first flight at eight weeks with no problems. When Ember came along about four years later, Tyler probably had more frequent flyer miles than the typical adult. Ember's first flight was at twelve weeks, and now at seven and three years old, they both have racked up miles and even have a couple of passport stamps. We've been blessed that travel is still a big part of our lives.

But providence wasn't the only reason we were able to continue to travel. It was written in our five-year vision and all over our vision boards, and we purposefully took the steps needed to achieve that vision. We traveled with our kids early in their lives to get them used to it and took them along on many adventures. Tyler attended his first concert at six months in Colorado, went to Grand Cayman Island, cruised to Mexico, snow skied in Colorado, and much more—all before his sister was born. Ember has had her fair share of adventures too, including seeing Niagara Falls, swimming in the Pacific and Atlantic Oceans, and visiting Legoland in California (twice). Everything was going great for a while. But then things changed.

Step One. Vision: We wanted the flexibility to travel without sacrificing the quality of our son's education.

When Tyler started kindergarten, our approach no longer worked. For the first time in our family life, we felt held back from traveling when and where we wanted to go. We had to plan around a school calendar, and we did not do very well. We maxed out the school's attendance policy days and traveled every time he was not in school, but by the end of the school year, we felt burned out. We decided there had to be a better solution. But to find it, we had to get clear about what we wanted. On a date, Mike and I got out a piece of paper and created a vision for our ideal situation. For schooling purposes, we wanted something that offered both the structure and flexibility we desired. Ideally, it would be a place that had a community feel like we had experienced with his preschool.

Step Two: Define what you need to do to start moving in that direction.

Once we defined what we wanted, we did some research and interviewed every school in our area. We asked the administrators the same question: "What if we wanted to spend the month of January in Colorado?" At each school we had the same reaction—they cringed! We had been considered homeschooling as an option, but with all our travel and work schedules, we didn't know how we'd achieve the structure we wanted to provide for Tyler's education.

Step Three: Track your progress.

We felt a little defeated but were reminded of a Thomas Edison quote, "When you have exhausted all possibilities, remember this—you haven't."

I had been part of a homeschooling moms group since Tyler was 18 months old. I picked the other moms' brains about their experiences, and one suggested we check out a place called Open Connections (www.openconnections.org). We looked it up online, and the more we read, the more excited we became.

It is a safe haven for families pursuing Partnership Education (often referred to as homeschooling or unschooling) to socialize, explore, and collaborate. Founded in 1975 on the belief that young people are born naturally curious about the world, Open Connections provides weekly programs for young people ages two to eighteen. The campus sits on a picturesque 28 acres, with woods, ponds and a creek, and offers ample opportunities for youth to engage in purposeful, hands-on experiences and activities. We set up a meeting with the directors to go see Open Connections first hand, and we fell in love with the place. Our son went for a trial day, and he too fell in love. For the remainder of that school year, he kept asking us when he would be able to back to Open Connections, and was so sad when we told him he had to wait until the following fall.

Step Four: Constantly update and evolve your approach.

Tyler has been at Open Connections since September 2015 and has loved every minute. We are truly living our vision of having a structured environment for the kids and one that is flexible so we can still travel when and where we'd like to go with no ill effects to their education. Without the clarity of vision, we may have settled for a less ideal option. However, this is not a one-time decision. Every year we will reevaluate whether this is still the course we want to take.

People often operate from a place of fear and the desire for comfort. It would have been much easier to simply fill out the paper work to send him back to his public school, but we would have had to give up one of the most important parts of our vision of the ideal family life. Because we were being purposeful, we took a leap of faith that has been very satisfying on so many levels.

I am not saying that Partnership Education/ homeschooling is right for every family, but I hope that sharing how we went from vision to reality in our own lives is helpful to you. When you are committed to your vision, it will come to fruition. There is a quote from T. S. Eliot on Tyler's homeschool planner that says, "Sometimes things become possible if we want them bad enough." When we make a commitment, we find a way to make it happen, even when we are afraid or uncomfortable.

Purposeful Parents Are Informed

When we brought our first child home from the hospital, we had no idea what we were doing. Sure, we had taken childbirth classes before they released us from the hospital, but truth be told, children don't come with an operations manual. Poor Tyler never had a real nap for the first six months of his life because I was under the impression that his bassinet should be reserved for bedtime only and that allowing him to nap there would confuse him. Mike went along not wanting to upset me and because he had no idea either. Tyler also ate baby puffs and yogurt drops for about a year because I was afraid he would choke on anything else.

There are so many things we do as parents out of fear, but when we start to look at the bigger picture, the vision for our family, the steps for getting there become more clear. I can't stress enough the importance of seeking advice from other parents, teachers, pediatricians, and other experts when you don't know what to do. One way to reduce your fear is to acquire knowledge. You can start by reading some of the books I recommended earlier. Expose yourself to new ways of thinking and see what works. As parents, our job is always changing. We are given only one year to parent our children as infants. Then we have to learn how to parent them as toddlers, then preschoolers, then school-aged, then tweens, and so on. On top of that, each child has their own unique set of challenges and opportunities. It is an ever-progressive experience that changes as soon as you feel you've mastered it. The key to adapting is being purposeful at each stage.

Instinctively as parents, we want our kids to grow up to be better off than we are, yet for many of us, we have no blueprint about how to do that. In his book *Greater Than Yourself: The Ultimate Lesson of True Leadership*, Steven Farber offers one to follow. He suggests that if you want to make someone greater than yourself, you first must expand yourself, then give of yourself, and ultimately replicate yourself. How many of us actually fear becoming our parents? Do you want your children to fear becoming you, or would you rather be someone they are proud of and look up to?

In my opinion, committing to the Miracle Morning practice has been the easiest and most effective way I have found to expand myself. Give yourself that hour, so you can successfully give your best self to your kids for the rest of the day. The next step is to give of yourself. So how do you do that purposefully? By being present.

Purposeful Parents Are Present Parents

In the book *The Available Parent: Expert Advice for Raising Successful, Resilient, and Connected Teens and Tweens*, Dr. John Duffy uses the phrase, "protecting time." This is exactly what we do when we wake up early to fit in our Miracle Morning. We're protecting time for ourselves to do the Life S.A.V.E.R.S.

As parents, we also need to protect the time we spend with our kids. If we are not purposeful about this, we'll end up losing our connection with our children. Research has shown that staying connected with your child is very important. According to the Education Training Research Associates:

Parent Child Connectedness (or PCC) is characterized by the quality of the emotional bond between parent and child and by the degree to which this bond is both mutual and sustained over time. When PCC is high in a family, the "emotional climate" is one of affection, warmth, satisfaction, trust, and minimal conflict. Parents and children who share a high degree of connectedness enjoy spending time together, communicate freely and openly, support and respect one another, share similar values, and have a sense of optimism about the future.

PCC has been called a "super-protector" as it has been linked to the prevention of such family challenges as drug use, violence, and unintended pregnancy in adolescents. As families become more pressed for time in our technology-riddled world, we need to be more purposeful about connecting with one another. Four of the easiest ways we have found to promote PCC in our home are:

1. don't overschedule
2. prioritize consistent family dinners
3. hold quarterly family board meetings with each child
4. stick to a bedtime ritual

1. Purposeful Parents Don't Overschedule Their Children

It's very important to pay attention to your children's stress levels. If you find that your child is stressed, you may be overscheduling. In his book *The Hurried Child: Growing Up Too Fast Too Soon*, David Elkind, PhD, explains that children today are stressed, and it's having devastating effects on them. He says kids are growing up too fast, too soon, and there are four main sources of hurrying: parents, schools, the media, and technology. Since this book is for parents, I am going to focus on this important relationship. Elkind says that parents hurry their children to grow up because of their own stressful lives, which he attributes to the rapid change in our society. Basically, we as parents need to get our stress under control so we can help our children do the same.

Elkind points to the serious effects of stress:

Just a few statistics help tell the tale. Infant mortality is up after more than a century of decline. More children are living in poverty today than two decades ago. There has been a fifty percent increase in obesity in children and adolescents over the last twenty years. Our teenage pregnancy rates are the highest for any Western society—twice that of England, which has the next highest rates. Suicide and homicide rates for teenagers are triple what they were twenty years ago. Educationally, SAT scores have plummeted, and at the other end, some fifteen to twenty percent of young children are "flunking" kindergarten. And perhaps most frightening of all, in the United States today, millions of children are being medicated to make them more tractable in school and at home. This is a several-hundred-fold increase over the last five years.

So, take a step back and do a stress inventory of your family life. In chapter 6, we talked about building an unwavering focus list by asking yourself three questions: What do you want to keep doing (or do more of)? What do you want to start doing? And what do you want to stop doing? Use these focus questions to see which activities you can cut out of your schedule. If it's something your kids can't live without but doesn't bring you joy, see if there is a carpool situation you can be part of or look for another creative solution. The bottom line is that doing too much is stressful to both parents and children, so by strategically eliminating activities that don't serve your family, you will create more space and freedom for everyone to enjoy their lives.

2. Family Dinners

One of the most common examples of protected time is the family dinner. It's also one of the most neglected time slots in our lives as families today. How often do we schedule things over the dinner hour? Or let other activities take priority during that time? Yet we know how important it is to reconnect with one another after a busy day, every day. Right?

Just in case you need more persuading, here are some of the statistics from a CASAColumbia study (2010) on the importance of family dinners:

- Teens who had frequent family dinners (five to seven per week) were more likely to report having high-quality relationships with their parents.

- Teens who had dinner with their families five or more times a week were almost twice as likely to receive A's in school compared to teens who had dinner with their families two or fewer times a week.

- The more often children had dinner with their parents, the less likely they were to smoke, drink, or use marijuana or other drugs.

- Children and adolescents who shared at least three meals with their family each week were 12 percent less likely to be overweight, 20 percent less likely to eat unhealthy foods, 35 percent less likely to develop an eating disorder, and 24 percent more likely to eat healthy foods.

- Students who regularly dine with parents are less likely to skip class.

- Seventy-two percent of teens believe eating together as a family is important.

- Sixty-two percent of teens who eat fewer than five meals with parents wish they could eat with their parents more often.

Sitting down to share a meal is so important for the communication in the family. To supercharge the family dinner, don't ask your kids how their day was or what they did at school, but go for specific and open-ended questions. For Christmas we bought the Melissa & Doug Family Dinner Box of Questions, which is great for this purpose. You can easily search the Internet for family dinner questions, and many options pop up. Simply get the words flowing. I'd also suggest having a no-electronics rule at the dinner table so everyone can be fully present with each other.

3. Quarterly Family Board Meetings

Another simple parent-child connectedness initiative we have implemented is called the Family Board Meeting. Jim Sheils, our friend and the author of *The Family Board Meeting* (and author of the foreword to this book), explains how important it is to schedule a four- to six-hour meeting with each one of your kids individually once a quarter. He suggests having a ritual where you (and your child if they have any) turn off the electronics. This is time directed by your child for the purpose of creating quality interactions with them and focusing on intentionally building your relationship together.

In the book, Jim lays out the three steps for a successful Board Meeting:

1. Be one-on-one with your child.
2. Have no electronics.
3. Do a fun activity of the child's choosing with *focused reflection*.

We book our Family Board Meetings on the same day, so Mike and Tyler will be together at the same time as Ember and I. Then the next time we switch so that each parent will have two meetings per quarter.

These meetings have been so memorable for our children and for us as parents. My first board meeting with Ember was to share her first manicure and a dinner date. I was shocked that she sat so still and loved every minute of having her nails painted. For their meeting, Mike took Tyler rock-climbing and to pick out a new two-wheeler bike, which he learned to ride that day. For Mike and Ember's first board meeting, they got dressed up, and he took her to see *The Nutcracker* ballet. Her eyes lit up when she saw the beautiful dancers on the stage, and Mike was able to witness and share in her joy. I took Tyler to a local indoor playground where we climbed and jumped and played together. Then we went out for a special lunch. The memories of these meetings will be cherished for years to come. At the end of each board meeting, we record the day's activities in a special journal, along with the answer to the question, "what was your favorite part of the day?"

Sometimes we get so crazy-busy in our lives that we forget to take time to do something fun with our kids. The quarterly family board meeting is time earmarked to let your kids lead you on an adventure and for you to reconnect with them. We schedule our dental appointments and doctor appointments way in advance. Why not schedule a date with your child? And keep that commitment no matter what. Our kids are our most important clients.

4. Bedtime Ritual

Another easy way to connect with your kids on a consistent basis is to have a bedtime ritual. Bedtime in our house starts an hour before it's time to get into bed. We turn off all electronics (because artificial light from screens interferes with melatonin, the sleep hormone), and the kids bathe and put their pajamas on. We dim the lights and focus on quieter activities, like playing games, building with blocks, working on art projects, putting together puzzles, or reading books. Once in bed, each of the kids gets a bedtime story, and we play a guided meditation for them.

The kids know what to expect each night for bedtime, which helps ease the transition from being awake to sleep. Most nights they fall asleep easily with no fanfare, which makes it much easier when it's our turn to turn in.

Your family's bedtime ritual will be different from ours, but the important thing is to be as consistent as possible. Good bedtime rituals for anyone include limiting exposure to bright lights and screens that emit blue light, which is especially disruptive to our circadian rhythm. There are special filters you can get for laptops and tablets if you have to work after dark, and we even have special night-lights for our kids that do not emit any low blue light (http://www.bulletproof.com/low-blue-nightlight). And remember what I shared in chapter 5 on Energy Engineering about the importance of getting enough sleep. Schedule everyone's bedtime so that they get the optimum amount of shut-eye each night.

Another great element to include in your bedtime ritual is reading. Studies show that learning is enhanced while you sleep, so reading something right before bed is a great thing to do. Eating a heavy meal or drinking caffeine right before bed is something to avoid, and adults should limit their alcohol intake because it can also disrupt sleep.

Purposeful Communication

Another way we can be purposeful parents is in the way we communicate with our kids. People in general do best when they know what is expected of them, and children are no different. It's our job as parents to clearly communicate our expectations to our kids.

In our household, we have created what we call the McCarthy Family Expectations. These apply to everyone in the household—not just the children. These are general principles for how we treat each other. I encourage you to come up with your own. When writing your standards, remember that wording is very important. Instead of a straight list of what not to do, write a list of what you can and will do. For example, instead of don't run in the house, you can say, please use your walking feet in the house.

Here is a model to start from:

1. When you make a mess, clean it up.

2. Please use your walking feet in the house.

3. Jumping is for trampolines only.

4. When you make a mistake, apologize and hug.

5. Violence towards one another will not be tolerated.

6. Remember to be polite. Manners go a long way to get you what you want.

7. Be respectful of one another.

8. Share toys not germs.

These guidelines come in handy for discipline purposes. Instead of doing time-outs in our house, when someone is not living up to the expectations, they are called out on it. We have these guidelines written on a whiteboard in our house, so when someone is not following them, we simply pull it out and remind them of the expectation. This way no one has to be the bad guy; it's a simple reminder of how we treat each other. The kids even call Mike and me out on occasion when we are out of line!

In addition to our expectations, we have created a family seal using our intentional family values. Using your written vision or your family vision board (or both) come up with a list of words that describe your ideal family life. If you're having a tough time coming up with words, you can Google family values for ideas. Once you have a pretty good list, start to narrow it down until you have just a few. It's great to get the whole family involved in this process. Everyone can contribute their own words, and if two or more have the same idea, that's probably a good one to include. Once you have your words you can create an image or an acronym to make it easy to remember.

Ours is called the McCarthy Family North Star. It consists of two triangles combined to create a six-sided star. In the center is Love, which is our underlying value. Each point of the star is another value: Adventure, Acceptance, Abundance, Creativity, Curiosity, and Contribution. We like math in our family, so we created this equation to remind us of our values: $Love = A^3 + C^3$

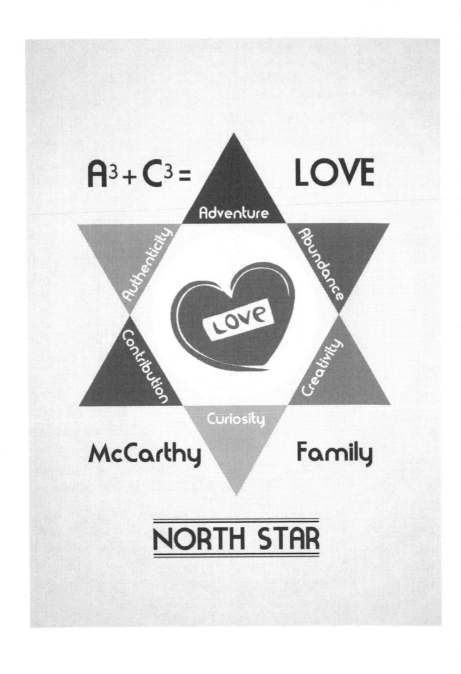

The other side of the communication coin is purposeful listening. We have to be willing to listen to our kids and be available for them to share their feelings. Lecturing and yelling at our kids is not effective communication. If we want them to listen to us, we first must listen to them and empathize with their feelings. Their issues may seem small to us, especially if we are under stress, but they are big and real to them. If we don't listen to them when their problems are small, it is unlikely that they will come to us with a big problem later on.

Practice intentional listening with your kids. Ask them a question and then wait for their reply. In the book *Fierce Conversations: Achieving Success at Work and in Life One Conversation at a Time* by Susan Scott, there is an idea that the quality of the relationship is connected to the quality of the questions you ask. Don't accept "I'm fine" as a final answer. Make eye contact and reflect back what you hear them saying and observe their body language. If your child is hesitant to talk with you, try asking questions in the car so they can avoid eye contact, or try asking when you are on a walk, playing a game, or working on an activity together. Make it a two-way conversation not an interrogation or a lecture. When we share our own vulnerabilities, our kids are much more willing to open up too.

Purposeful Partnerships

In parenting it is impossible to do it all yourself. Parents always intend the best for their kids, but that doesn't mean we always know the best way to do certain things. To truly provide our kids with the best life has to offer, we sometimes need to take a back seat and let them learn from the masters. This is where purposeful partnerships come into play. Here are two examples that illustrate the point. When it's time to get my car fixed, I go to a mechanic, and when I'm sick, I go to a doctor. I am not well-versed in car repair and Internet searches of medical conditions often leave me thinking I'm dying. It's important to seek professionals for specific help and support.

Asking for Help

If your child is interested in computer programming, but you have no idea how to program a computer, you can help them find the information or point them to someone who might have the required expertise. In the age of technology, it's so easy to find people with the knowledge we desire. Similarly, if your child loves music, but that is not your talent, help them find a great music teacher. The easiest way to master anything in life is to find someone doing what you'd like to do and follow their lead. If you can't be the model for your child in a certain area, then help them find a mentor. Knowing the right information, however, is only part of the equation. You want to make sure that there is a real connection between your child and their teachers. If you discover that your child is not enthusiastic or engaged by a particular teacher, continue searching until you find someone who is a great match.

We can help design our child's future by shaping the type of people in their lives. The great motivational speaker Jim Rohn famously said, "You are the average of the five people you spend the most time with." This concept is based on the law of averages, which is the theory that the result of any given situation will be the average of all outcomes. When children are young, they may spend the most time with a daycare teacher, nanny, or perhaps a relative. How purposeful are you about selecting those people? Who are you purposefully surrounding your children with?

Hiring Help

In business there is a mantra that goes like this: slow to hire, quick to fire. I have adopted this when hiring anyone who will care for our kids. To me, our kids are the most important thing in the world, so I take my time when hiring someone who will care for them. I need babysitters in my life so that I can accomplish everything I want to do and have time to recharge. Our babysitters have become part of our family, so I take their selection very seriously. I also like to hire babysitters who are ambitious, so I realize up front they are not going to be with us forever. This is why I have developed a purposeful system to screen candidates and to search for talent continually.

The interview process is much like a business interview. I have had great success using Care.com to find our babysitters. Additional sources include referrals from friends, classifieds, babysitting co-ops among friends, and placement services. The key is to make the search top of mind and to strategically identify your best options. Through trial and error, I have found that the more specific I am about the job opportunity, the more aligned the responses will be. For example, I knew I would need help to pick Tyler up from school three days a week, and I included that detail in the description so that the expectations were clear up front. This weeded out those who could not commit to that time frame or did not have reliable transportation.

After I receive some responses, I schedule a 20-minute phone interview with each candidate to conduct a quick initial screening. The purpose of this call is to determine whether they are a match for the job profile and if I feel a connection to them. If I feel optimistic about the person and their qualifications, then I invite them to take a simple personality assessment called the DISC (which they can take for free online- https://www.123test.com/disc-personality-test). I explain that it helps me get to know them better before we meet, and I ask them to forward me the results before the meeting.

The assessment serves two purposes. The obvious one is that it reveals their behavior and this lets me know if the applicant is a good match for our family. The second purpose is to see how responsible they are and whether they can correctly follow directions. Right away, if they don't send the results to me, it tells me *something* about them. I give everyone the benefit of the doubt, so if I was really impressed by the candidate on the phone, then I will still meet with them and have them take the assessment during the meeting.

I schedule the interviews during a time when the kids are home so I can see how they will interact with the potential sitter. During the interview, I ask all kinds of questions, but I am basically trying to find out if the person is someone I want in our kids' lives and the possible value they will bring to our kids that I might not be able to provide. For example, our current babysitter is a speech pathology major and knows sign language. She has been teaching the kids some simple signs. When they teach the signs to Mike and me, it brings them great joy. If you have ever thought, *I don't have any great help with childcare,* it may be that you haven't been purposeful in your search. It takes effort and focus on the front end, but like any system, it pays dividends in the form of freedom in the long run.

Partnership with Friends

As your kids grow into school age, they will start spending more of their time with their peers than with adults. While you can't pick their friends for them, you can certainly get to know their friends. You can also be choosy about whom you spend your time with and model healthy relationships. Mike and I seek out like-minded individuals to be in our lives, and our kids get the benefit of becoming friends with our friend's children.

Mike and I have friends all over the country, so no matter where we travel, our kids have built-in playmates. Locally, we have a strong group of friends, and even though all our kids go to different schools, they still get together regularly to play, and they have literally grown up with each other. You can open your home and heart to your children's friends by creating a safe, fun, and welcoming place to play. Offer to host their friends and get to know them. Invite them to dinner. Agree to carpool to soccer, tae kwon do, dance, or other activities. Ask their friends questions and then be a great listener. Engage with them. This will model healthy relationships for your children, and you will also learn useful information about your child's life, who their friends are, and discover if their family values are aligned with yours. Also, you never know what you might learn about your own child through their friend's perspective. All of this will help you curate better partnerships for your family.

The Importance of a Working Partnership with your Partner

The most important partnership, in my opinion, is the one with your partner. I think it is vital to put that relationship in the first position. When the partnership between the parents is not a strong, united front, kids pick up on it and will pit you against each other. Children are master negotiators and seek to meet their needs and wants, even if it creates conflict. This is not their fault. Kids' brains are still developing, and you cannot expect them to understand adult relationships.

It is our responsibility as parents to model love and respect for our children. The best way to do this is to take care of the relationship with your partner purposefully.

Here are a few suggestions for purposeful actions to help nurture and strengthen your marriage:

- Protect time with your partner. Make time to go on regular date nights and even vacations *without* your kids.

- Express gratitude for each other every day. In your journal write three things you love and appreciate about your partner and share that with them before part in the morning. It may be as simple as "I am grateful that you took the trash out last night so I didn't have to" or as big as "I appreciate that you are a great provider for our family."

- Show generosity and kindness to each other every day. Keep romance alive by leaving love notes for your spouse or surprising them with a small, thoughtful gift.

- Create a set of relationship values. F.R.E.S.H. is an acronym for our relationship values. It stands for Fun, Respectful, Enthusiastic, Supportive and Harmonious. These values guide the way we treat each other. I'd encourage you to create your own with your partner.

- Seek marriage counseling when needed. If you've hit a problem that you can't seem to get past, there is no shame in calling in a professional. This can be a very important partnership as well. Mike and I actually created F.R.E.S.H. during a counseling session.

- Build a group of friends in which you can confide so that you're not depending on your spouse for all of your support. Your spouse and children cannot be your whole world. Find like-minded people you can spend time with who bring you joy and purposely schedule time with them. For example, Mike is part of a men's mastermind group called GoBundance (www.gobundance.com), and I am committed to monthly girls nights that I organize with friends.

- Talk about problems rather than suffering in silence. Your spouse cannot read your mind. If you are having a problem, share it with them.

- Look for solutions that work for both partners. Always look for a win-win resolution.

- Have a word or phrase for taking a time-out when things get heated. Ours is "inner-mission."

- Share your visions and goals with each other.

- Be clear and open in your communication. The system Mike and I use is to protect time each week to have a family meeting to discuss the calendar, our finances, and anything else we need the other's input on. We also check in at the end of each day to reflect and prepare for the next one.

- Sometimes situations arise when your love relationship has ended with the other person, but you can still model love through acceptance. Often times in relationships people will tolerate poor behavior, cheating, or abuse and try to stick it out for the kids, but that is not modeling love. If this is your situation, it's better to love yourself enough to move on and find someone more deserving of your love. To tolerate bad behavior from a spouse or partner only enables them to keep making poor choices. It is better to get out of a toxic relationship.

Kids as Partners

Kids also make great partners. When you enlist your child's help with a problem or a project, it can have a powerful effect on their confidence level and strengthen the their sense of value as a family member. Look for ways to involve your child as a partner. You'll be glad you did.

For example, Tyler loves to use a big knife, so when preparing dinner, I allow him chop all the vegetables. He feels good because he contributes to putting dinner on the table, and it takes less time to make the meal. He had a learning curve in the beginning, but now that he knows how to use a knife, he no longer needs supervision, and dinner takes less time. Ember is now learning to use a knife too, so she gets things like olives and avocados to cut with a butter knife.

As we mentioned earlier, another time to enlist your children's help is when coming up with your family's values. The more you involve the kids in this process, the more buy-in you will get from them, which leads to increased cooperation.

Final Thoughts on Purposeful Parenting

Being a purposeful parent is about getting clear on your family's vision, your expectations and values, your partnerships, and in your communication. Remember, to make your kids greater than yourself, you first need to expand yourself into the person you want your children to look up to by practicing the Life S.A.V.E.R.S. daily. Next, you need to give yourself to your children by protecting time with them to connect on a deep level. As parents, we should know our children better than anyone else. Lastly, model healthy partnerships for your children and teach them your family vision and values. When you become intentional parents, your children's early lives are no longer left to luck or chance but are carefully cocreated on purpose.

PARENTING PROFILE

PAT FLYNN

Pat is an entrepreneur, blogger, and podcaster known for his Smart Passive Income website, where he shares the results of his income experiments. The *Smart Passive Income Podcast* is consistently ranked in the top 10 podcasts in the iTunes Business category.

Pat is married and has two children, a son age 7 and a daughter age 3.

How has The Miracle Morning changed your family life?

I used to be a night owl, but I started to see some pretty immediate changes when I shifted to the Miracle Morning. For one, I was just in a better mood. Two, I felt a lot more energized when I was working. After some physical activity, some meditation, and some gratitude, I could start the day out fresh. I felt that my work was a lot more meaningful. Because I'm in a better mood, I can become a better parent. I can be 100 percent focused on the kids.

Best Parenting Tips

Practice gratitude and teach it to your kids. If my kids are up, they're watching me do the Life S.A.V.E.R.S., and I talk to them about what I'm grateful for and why that's important. At different times throughout the day, I ask my kids to tell me what they're thankful for to get them in the habit.

Maintaining a healthy perspective. A lot of parents ask themselves, "Why me? Other people's kids don't do this. Why is this happening?" I try to remind myself that you can't stop your kids' behavior, but you can control how you react to it. The way that I react when they're rowdy is how they're going to react when other people aren't behaving the way that they want. I always try to lead by example.

Create a community with other parents. It's very important to have other parents you can consult and trade stories with. That community aspect is crucial for support. My wife and I are really lucky because a lot of our friends have kids the same age as ours.

Meditation tip for parents. I use a device called the Muse to help me meditate. It's a headband with sensors on it that can read your brain activity. It connects to an app called Calm on your phone, which can tell you when you are in a meditative state.

Present a unified front. Once my wife makes a decision to do something, even if I do not agree, we don't disagree in front of the kids. We never say, "Oh, he didn't deserve that." We talk about those things afterwards in private and are very open with each other then.

Be playful. We enjoy role playing. We let our kids choose a scenario, and then they tell us how to be actors in those scenes. We just let them have free rein sometimes. I think that makes it really fun because when they see a big adult on all fours acting like an elephant, it's playtime. In the beginning, I struggled with getting comfortable being silly, but I found out that the sillier I am, the more hugs I receive and the closer I get to them. That's because I'm speaking their language.

Use a schedule. I've started actually scheduling things that are in my Miracle Morning because I found that when things are in the calendar, they get done. Put it up there as high on your list as possible so that when you do have time, you get back into it and don't let it slip.

Final Word

The golden rule still applies. It's similar to what I teach in business. Your earnings are a byproduct of how well you serve your audience. I tell my kids, "What you give the world, the world gives back to you." So let's give the world great things. Let's treat people with kindness, and they will treat us with kindness, too.

PARENTING PROFILE
MARY LYNN SNOW

Mary Lynn is a full-time nurse manager and is the mother of three children, two sons, ages 7 and 2, and a daughter age 5. Mary Lynn's husband, Ryan Snow, cowrote *The Miracle Morning for Salespeople*.

On sharing the Miracle Morning with kids.

Our older son is a great participant in the Miracle Morning. He has written his affirmations and is becoming proud and confident by saying them every day. If Ryan and I are reading or meditating, he'll join in for those things or exercise. That's one he really enjoys. This past week right when he woke up, he jumped right in and started exercising in the middle of our routine. It was comical, actually!

Best Parenting Tips

Don't forget playfulness. I work full-time, so when I come home, I try to dedicate time just for them, be it playing before bedtime or reading at night before they go to sleep. Just giving them that quality time, whatever that looks like, is how we incorporate playfulness with them.

Use positive discipline. If our children have something unkind to say, or if they get in trouble, we have them do "I am" statements. We do one "I am" statement for every year of age. I think it's actually made a really positive change for them. For example, if our son was being rude to his sister, we'd have him say, "I am kind" seven times.

Spend one-on-one time with the kids. Generally, we'll dedicate a date night. So I'll take one child, and Ryan will stay with the other two to continue that one-on-one interaction with them. We want them to know that they're special to us and they're getting that quality time.

Be purposeful. The Miracle Morning has made us more organized, calmer, and more patient, so that helps us to be purposeful in parenting our children. It has also helped us to remember that they're always learning and growing.

Each child is unique. Kids are still learning, so being really harsh with them or giving lots of punishments is not the right way. We try to keep that in mind, that each of our children is unique, and we need to treat them as such. Their learning styles are different from each other's, so what works for one might not work for another.

Find good resources. One book that I read and really enjoyed that described my oldest child perfectly is, *Raising Your Spirited Child: A Guide for Parents Whose Child Is More Intense, Sensitive, Perceptive, Persistent, and Energetic* by Mary Sheedy Kurcinka. My son is really energetic, and he learns a little differently than other kids. The book will remind you that you're not the only one with a spirited child, so you're not the only one struggling. It will make you feel supported.

Create healthy partnerships. I think my most important partnership is with Ryan. A lot of it is impromptu. The kids will go to bed, and we'll evaluate how the day went. If there are things we could have done better, if there were opportunities for improvement during the day, we'll make a plan going forward, which is always important. It's good to talk about it, but then you need an action plan. So, we do a lot of that, but we also nurture our relationship through date nights and an occasional night away, which has been great. Without the two of us being on the same page, the family unit can't function appropriately.

Talk about money. We talk about bank accounts, saving money, and being purposeful with how we're spending it with our seven-year-old, but we could be better at it, and we are seeking ways to improve that right now.

Kids are resilient. One of our great accomplishments was supporting our older son as he learned to ride a bike. He fell down countless times. But he just kept trying. After three to four days, he could finally ride that bike, and he was so proud! It was amazing to watch his resilience.

Parenting Success Story

Our son has a panic disorder. It was affecting his social life and his day-to-day skills of being able to go to school. Together, Ryan and I put a plan in place to get him some counseling. The meditation and the affirmations have helped a lot, too. It helps to ground him. He has a lot of energy, so putting the whole puzzle together with some traditional and some nontraditional care has helped settle him, and he actually hasn't had a panic attack in over a year!

Final Word

I just want to say to any parent out there that you're not alone. I felt alone when I started going through some of these difficulties with my son, when he was having panic attacks. Then he went to school, and they didn't think he would be able to read, and now he's excelling in reading. You're not alone. Reach out to your school or your community. There's always someone there to help you, to refocus you, and to support you.

— 8 —
EXCEPTIONAL PARENTING SKILL #2:
PLAYFULNESS

Play is often talked about as if it were a relief from serious learning. But for children play is serious learning. Play is really the work of childhood.
—Fred Rogers, Iconic actor from Mr. Rogers' Neighborhood

When was the last time you were playful with your kids? As adults, we can get so wrapped up in our work, running the household, making sure the kids are signed up for all the right after-school activities, and being the scout leader and soccer coach, that we leave little time for play. But we all know that play has an important role in the development of healthy children. Young children learn social skills and fine and gross motor skills through play. They develop problem-solving skills, critical thinking, and creativity. They explore their world through play—and it is also important for adults!

In his book *Play: How it Shapes the Brain, Opens the Imagination and Invigorates the Soul*, Stuart Brown, MD, says, "Play is a state of mind, rather than an activity. Remember the definition of play: an absorbing, apparently purposeless activity that provides enjoyment and a suspension of self-consciousness and sense of time. It is self-motivating and makes you want to do it again. We have to put ourselves in the proper emotional state in order to play." What's play to one person may be hard work to another. You may get great joy out of gardening, while someone else may find it to be pure torture. That means we all need to define what play is for ourselves. One thing's for certain, you will feel amazing when you experience true play.

The Many Benefits of Play

It's no secret that play has many powerful benefits, for both kids and adults. It's been shown to release endorphins in the body that produce an overall feeling of well-being and can even temporarily reduce physical pain. Play can improve brain function. Games like chess or puzzles challenge the brain and utilize memory. When we look at a problem with a playful state of mind, we often find innovative solutions. As Einstein said, "We can't solve problems by using the same kind of thinking we used when we created them."

When playing with others, we strengthen our connections with them. Being playful can help to break the ice with strangers as well as add humor to an otherwise stressful situation. Play boosts your energy and vitality and even improves your resistance to disease, helping you feel your best. In the words of George Bernard Shaw, "We don't stop playing because we grow old; we grow old because we stop playing."

And it may surprise you that play is a vital ingredient in healthy relationships. Young children will behave like the adults in their lives. If we keep things light, our kids will too. But if we're constantly stressed around our kids and fighting with our spouse, they will adopt that behavior instead. We need to be playful not only with our children, but also with our partner. Just as playing with our kids will help their development and create a long-lasting bond, playing with your spouse will keep your relationship fresh and deepen intimacy. The bottom line is, play is fun, and if we allow ourselves the opportunity, it can be massively enjoyable.

Tips for High-Quality Playtime with Your Kids

Play comes in all forms. Independent play for children is as important as playing with kids their own age. And having fun with their parents helps to foster that relationship, which is so essential.

Here are some helpful tips to encourage play with your children:

1. **Create regular play times.** Get into the habit of playing with your kids daily or at a regular time each week. For example, Mike plays with the kids after dinner every night for 30 minutes while I decompress and clean up the kitchen. The kids know to expect this time with their dad and look forward to it each day.

2. **Get rid of distractions.** Put down the cell phone, turn the TV off, and step away from the computer. When we give our kids our undivided attention, they feel special.

3. **Don't force it.** Play ceases to be play when it is forced. If your child isn't having fun with an activity, do something else. Rules don't always need to be followed. If you're playing a board game, and your child is having a hard time, create new rules.

4. **Repetition is a good thing.** Young children especially love to read the same book or play the same game over and over. It might not be your idea of a good time, but it's helping your child learn and developing a loving relationship with you, so embrace it! They won't want to play Candy Land forever.

5. **Let your children take the lead.** Instead of trying to control their play, jump into it. If your child loves to pretend, let them tell you who you are and ask them questions so they can create the scene. Let them make the rules and determine the pace. Ember loves to play the mom and tell us we are the kids. It's fun to reverse roles.

6. **Get dirty.** Go ahead and sit on the floor, run around in the rain, or get grass stains. Mirror your child's play: if they are rolling on the floor, do it too. If they get loud, match their intensity. As long as no one is getting hurt, it's okay to be energetic and get dirty!

7. **Play it safe.** It's all fun and games until someone gets hurt. If there are any safety rules to a game or required equipment, make sure the children understand that so you can prevent injuries. For example, if you're at a park with swings, remind your child not to walk too closely. Or if your child wants to ride bikes, make sure they wear a helmet.

8. **Age-appropriate play.** If something is too challenging or too easy, your child will quickly lose interest. However, when you play with kids of different ages, keep games geared toward the youngest. If a game is too hard for them, it will often result in tears, which is no fun for anyone.

It's never too late to revert to your childhood days and enjoy some good old-fashioned fun. As children, we all played naturally. So amidst all the adult concerns you have, don't forget to practice playfulness. As many of the parents I interviewed for this book have pointed out, playing with your kids is the easiest way to get back in the swing of lightheartedness.

In the last few years, coloring books have been created for adults, and they have been selling like mad. Brianna Greenspan created an amazing hybrid coloring book—for adults and children—titled The Miracle Morning *Art of Affirmations: A Positive Coloring Book for Adults & Kids*, which is made up of positive affirmations that parents can color with their kids. You can then cut them up on a vision board, or hang them on your walls. It's a great way to get your kids engaged with you in creating and repeating affirmations, and is available now on Amazon.com.

The need for play in adults is not obvious. It is similar to the need for rest that we discussed in chapter 5 on energy engineering. Yet the research is clear that play is important for adults. We need to lighten up, stop fearing what others will think, and enjoy the time we have here on Earth.

One of the most fun times I can recall with Tyler was during a party we hosted at our home. We ordered a moon bounce slide for the kids to enjoy during the party, but it was pouring rain, and no one had their bathing suits or a change of clothes. Tyler was sad that he wasn't going to get to play on it. I excused myself from my hostess duties and told Tyler to go get his bathing suit on. I got my bathing suit on too, and we had a ball playing on our giant, personal water slide. When we'd had our fill and came back to the party, several people commented about the pure joy on our faces. We truly had lost track of time and were fully living in the moment, not worrying about what any of the party guests were thinking. It was clear that we wanted to be out in the rain creating that memory together.

Energetic Connection

A playful mindset will help you loosen up. As adults, we often either live in the past or worry about the future. We hurry and then hurry our children. We leave little time to be flexible. The younger your kids are, the more present they are, and the more connected they are to you. Children are energetically attached to their parents until they are about the age of two.

Try this experiment: At Christmastime, scan your Facebook feed. Look at the expressions on the children's faces as they sit on Santa's lap. If the child is under two, I can almost guarantee that the child is not happy. Why? Chances are the parents handing the child over are nervous. They are scared the baby will cry and ruin the picture and, therefore, the Christmas cards. Or they are annoyed they had to wait in line so long, or they are worried about the germs Santa might pass on to their bundle of joy. Whatever emotions they are feeling, the baby is feeling them too. At about age three, the pictures change, and the kids are grinning from ear to ear because they finally grasp that the guy in the big red suit brings them presents!

Because children, especially the littlest ones, are so connected to their parents, reserving time for your Miracle Morning practice can be quite challenging. As soon as you start waking up earlier to get your Life S.A.V.E.R.S. in, chances are, your child will be right behind you. So what is a well-intended parent to do? The short answer is stay flexible, be playful, and remember that this too shall pass.

Finding a Creative Solution

When I committed to the Miracle Morning, I was pumped. I set my alarm clock early, I got up and did my Life S.A.V.E.R.S., and I felt unstoppable—until a week later when our youngest started coming in and interrupting me. My first response was to sit her in front of the TV so I could finish my Miracle Morning in peace. Huge mistake! Yes, I was able to finish in peace, but afterwards all hell broke loose as I tried to get her away from the TV set and ready for the day ahead. My next idea was to let her play quietly in the room with me as I did my practice. This worked much better. Yes, she would still interrupt, but I explained to her what I was doing and that, if she wanted to stay with me, she would have to play on her own while I finished up.

This was working out! Once I took TV time off the table, and she grew bored playing by herself each morning, she returned to her more typical wake time. I discovered a side benefit that I hadn't anticipated. She started asking questions about what I was doing and, more importantly, WHY? This gave me the opportunity to practice articulating exactly why I was doing it (especially since she asked at least a few times each morning).

Once the kids saw how much more playful and patient I became with them as a result of the growth from doing my Life S.A.V.E.R.S., they wanted to be a part of it too. I started slowly with them. At first I simply explained what each of the Life S.A.V.E.R.S. meant and allowed them to do what they wanted from them. I used the poems I had written in the middle of the night that I mention in the introduction of this book to help them understand. I didn't want to overwhelm them or for it to feel like a chore. I wanted it to be fun for them and for it eventually to be something they chose to do on their own.

Now our kids have been doing the Miracle Morning for almost a year, and our oldest (at age seven) has progressed to the point that he only needs reminding, and our three-year-old daughter still needs us to actively participate in most of her activities.

C.H.A.R.M.S.

After about a month of doing Life S.A.V.E.R.S., Tyler asked, "Mommy, why do I need to save my life?" I explained that, when Hal wrote *The Miracle Morning*, he literally used these practices to save his life, and that is why he called it the Life S.A.V.E.R.S. Tyler was having a hard time connecting with the acronym, so as Hal suggests in *The Miracle Morning*, we customized it to fit Tyler's needs. Tyler and I got out a piece of scrap paper and wrote out all the words in Life S.A.V.E.R.S. then started playing with them.

Since Ember didn't know her letters yet, we had been using creativity for scribing, so we started there: C for creativity. Affirmations in our opinion couldn't be changed, so we kept A for affirmations. Like most kids, ours have a hard time with silence, and most of their visualization was done through guided meditations. So we decided to combine silence and visualization into one category called meditation: M for meditation. We expanded the exercise to include a healthy breakfast. So we renamed it health: H for health. We wanted to keep it at six letters, so we added an S for service because it is something important to us that we wanted to instill in our children.

After unscrambling the letters, we came up with the Life C.H.A.R.M.S. Tyler was so happy with the new acronym. He had helped to create his own Miracle Morning routine, and he couldn't wait to get started! Involving the kids in their own Miracle Morning so that they could have a morning ritual too was the solution we found to interruptions.

If you try this practice with your children, remember to be flexible and forgiving with yourself and them. It's not about perfection. It's about priming your kids so they will *want* to do it on their own. We do not wake our kids up early to do their Miracle Morning but have them do it once they wake on their own. If your children are older, they can make the choice to wake up early to complete their Life C.H.A.R.M.S., but I wouldn't encourage you to force them to do it. Our kids always have the choice to do them or not, but they are not allowed any screen time until all six are completed. Some days it takes them all day to complete their Miracle Morning!

Creativity

C is for Creativity. Use your imagination to create something new.

Make a creation.

It is what we came to do.

What's inside of you?

Observe your children. What's play to them? What's more like work? When you become aware of their interests, you can guide them to activities they will happily take part in independently. For Ember, it's pretend play. She will joyfully play with a dollhouse, stuffed animals, her play kitchen, or pretend makeup for some time by herself. Tyler is more of an experiential learner. For him, it's Legos, outdoor play, puzzles, drawing, or making things. For your kids, it might be playing music, singing, writing, or art. As long as they use their minds to do or create something they love, it counts! Once they get the hang of it, they may make new discoveries and expand their interests, discovering many new things that they want to explore. This is all perfectly natural and creative.

I've talked a lot about increasing playfulness in this chapter. Play fuels creativity and vice versa. When we allow our kids to have a safe space for their creative expression, passions will be born. Let them find their flow deep in their imaginations.

Health

H is for Health. Move your body and fill it with healthy foods.

Health is all about

your body. Move it, shake it,

fill it with goodness.

As I've discussed already, exercise is crucially important for good health, and nutrition is equally essential. With childhood obesity on the rise and families living a more rushed lifestyle, kids are not getting what they need nutritionally. Starting their day with a meal that is high in protein has been shown to help them feel full longer and eat fewer calories at lunchtime. It also prevents body fat increases, reduces cravings for sweets later in the day, and stabilizes glucose levels in the body. So bring on the eggs and bacon and skip the high sugar and carbohydrate cereals and pastries. A study of 5,000 kids (ages 9–11) by Cardiff University showed that children are twice as likely to score higher than average grades if they start the day with a healthy breakfast. An Australian survey of over 500 teachers revealed that students lose two hours of learning a day if they skip breakfast because of the inability to concentrate and behavior problems related to hunger. Research supports the fact that eating breakfast is a great idea!

When it comes to exercise and kids, it's important to keep it fun and not to overdo it. Kids' bones are still growing, so they don't need to lift weights. In our house we like to play games that involve exercise. For example, we play Red Light, Green Light or Simon Says with the younger one. Tyler loves it when we set up obstacle courses for him to complete. We also invested in a couple mini trampolines, so the kids can jump to their hearts' content without ruining our furniture. If you know your child has an activity coming up, like gym class, soccer practice, or dance class, be sure to make the morning exercise something light and fun just to get their blood pumping. If possible, have them do their exercise outside to get the bonuses of vitamin D and fresh air.

Exercise can also be great for family bonding. We pride ourselves on living a very active lifestyle, and we have not allowed having kids to be an excuse for becoming less so. As Jim Rhon says, "If you don't take care of your body, where are you going to live?"

On weekends, when we have more time, we like to do our exercise as a family. Mike organizes an ultimate frisbee game once a month, and we bring the kids along to join in the fun. We also like to hike and bike together or go kayaking as a family. Ember is still a little young, but Tyler attends cardio classes with me at the gym (and he generally works harder than the adults in the class). Yoga is also a great family exercise. Even babies can be incorporated into poses. There is a series on YouTube called Cosmic Kids Yoga that is wonderful.

Affirmations

A is for affirmation. That is a positive I AM statement.

Affirmation is

a big word for shouting out

who I choose to be.

I believe it's best to keep affirmations short for younger children. Simple, positive *I am* statements work wonderfully. Help your children create their own affirmation books in their own words. For the first month or so, this was Tyler's creativity portion of the Life C.H.A.R.M.S. He followed the alphabet and chose a word for each letter that resonated with him and then drew a picture representing the word. Because she's younger, Ember needed more help with hers. I chose the words for her, and she has yet to complete all the drawings, but every child works at their own pace. As your kids get older and start setting their own goals, you can assist them in creating affirmations to support their specific ambitions following the formula in the Life S.A.V.E.R.S. section of this book.

There are some great children's books that teach about the power of affirmations. Some of my favorites include the following:

- *I Think, I Am! Teaching Kids the Power of Affirmations* by Louise Hay

- *Unstoppable Me! 10 Ways to Soar Through Life* by Dr. Wayne W. Dyer and Kristina Tracy

- *I AM a Lovable ME! (I Am a Lovable Me!)* by Sharon R. Penchina and Stuart Hoffman

- *Just Because I Am: A Child's Book of Affirmation* by Lauren Murphy Payne, MSW, (author) and Claudia Rohling, MSW, (illustrator)

I also discovered a personalized affirmations book from UncommonGoods.com It's called *M is for Me* and you can order one with your child's name on the cover.

Sometimes the kids give me a hard time about saying their affirmations, so here are some things I've learned through trial and error. Have them "echo" their affirmations. You say it first, and they repeat what you say. Try using funny voices or a puppet. They can sing their affirmations to the tune of "If You're Happy and You Know It," but change the words to match their affirmations. For example, if the affirmation is I am grateful, they can sing, "If you're grateful and you know it say I'm grateful … I'm grateful, etc." There are also recorded songs you can download that include affirmations in the lyrics. Some examples include: "Grateful" by Brotha James, "Radiate" by Jack Johnson, "Living in the Moment" by Jason Mraz, "I am the Light of My Soul" by Snatam Kaur, "We are Okay" by Joshua Radin, "What a Wonderful World" by Louis Armstrong, "Imagine" by John Lennon, "Don't Worry, Be Happy" by Bobby McFerrin, "Man in the Mirror" by Michael Jackson, and many more. Remember to be creative, playful, and flexible. If all else fails, try again later or tomorrow!

Reading

R is for reading. What story will you read today?

A book in my hand;

Reading is an adventure

I can have again …

and again and again and again!

Reading is pretty self-explanatory, but if your child isn't reading independently yet, you or an older sibling can help them with this one. Another option is audiobooks. In our house, no screen time is allowed until all the Life C.H.A.R.M.S. are finished, but listening to a story or a guided meditation are the exceptions. Reading is the cornerstone for learning, and studies show that reading to your child from birth will give them great advantages. It is important to read with your child, even if they already know how to read independently. Here are some benefits that will come from reading together:

- **Hold on to childhood:** As cliché as it is, kids grow up so fast! Newborns quickly turn into babies, who turn into toddlers, who go off to preschool, and then you blink, and they are off to college. Take advantage of the time when they are young and will cuddle up on the couch to read a book with you. If you make this a regular activity, it becomes a tradition of relaxing and spending time together.

- **Educational boost:** One of the main advantages of reading to toddlers and preschoolers is that it creates a stronger propensity for learning in general. Studies show that when adults read to young children before they start school, they are more likely to do well in all areas of formal schooling.

- **Basic speech skills.** Listening to language is one of the most important activities babies can have. Young children can understand language at a much higher level than they can express. When you read to your preverbal child, you help them develop critical language and enunciation skills. As they listen, they are learning. Eventually they will start to "read" along with books they have heard many times before, and preschoolers can start sounding out words on their own.

- **Understanding their environment.** Even the smartest baby does not understand how a book works. As you read with your child on your lap, they get the idea that the words on the page represent something. They learn that text and pictures are separate, and if you run your finger along while you read, they will understand that words flow from left to right. These are all essential pre-reading skills.

- **Improved social skills.** Many books for young children introduce them to acceptable social behavior and show them how to express themselves to others in healthy ways. Kids learn how to share and have compassion and empathy from seeing how the characters in a book interact with each other. Asking questions about the book as you read keeps the child engaged and helps them to take lessons from the story.

- **Added logical thinking skills.** As your toddler or preschooler begins to relate what they hear in books to what's happening in their own world, they become more excited about the stories you share. Reading to children increases their ability to grasp abstract concepts, apply logic in various scenarios, recognize cause and effect, and use good judgment.

- **Faster acceptance of new experiences.** When your child is young, they will have many first experiences. They usually start school or daycare, which can be scary for them. If we can help them understand the process through a story, they might not have as much resistance to a new situation. Check your local library for books to help ease their minds about going to the dentist, visiting with relatives, going on a plane, and so on.

- **Better focus and discipline.** Young children may squirm and become distracted during story time, but eventually they'll come to enjoy this activity and sit for the entire session. A longer attention span leads to improved reading comprehension, better self-discipline, and stronger memory retention, all of which will serve your child in an educational setting.

- **Understanding that reading is fun!** The sooner you start reading to your child, the quicker they will learn that reading is not a chore. Kids who are read to as babies are much more likely to choose books over other forms of entertainment when they start reading independently.

Don't stop the activity once your child is reading independently. On average, kids' reading levels don't catch up to their listening levels until eighth grade. When we read with our older kids, we can help them tackle problems before they face them in real life. For example, your child may be headed to middle school next year and will face switching classrooms and keeping a locker. You could read a book together about someone in that situation and then ask questions about what you read. This is a much better tactic than lecturing, which your child will ignore.

As Jim Trelease, the author of *The Read-Aloud Handbook*, explains "When you talk about a book together, it's not a lecture, it's more like a coach looking at a film with his players, going over the plays to find out what went right and what went wrong." It can also be a great way to bond over shared interests. Before we travel, we like to read books about where we are going to the kids. When we get there, they already know a little about the destination.

Meditation

M is for meditation. Quiet down and be still.

Meditation is

not hard. Simply breathe in deep

and quiet your mind.

The Dalai Lama said, "If every 8-year-old in the world is taught meditation, we will eliminate violence from the world within one generation." I agree wholeheartedly with him and also believe you can start much younger than age eight. I started my meditation journey around the time Tyler was a baby. I would often meditate while feeding him, and Mike started meditating with him at bedtime around age three. Soon after those bedtime meditations started, Mike asked Tyler what it was like for him to meditate, and he replied, "My brain starts glowing, and then it explodes, and I grow a new one." Kids innately understand meditation. To them, it's not something weird or complicated; it's easy and natural. The younger your kids are, the faster they will catch on to meditation.

The easiest way to get started with meditation is through a guided or active meditation. YouTube is a great resource for free children's guided meditations. With guided meditation, the conscious mind is given a job to do (visualize or focus on a mantra or your breath) that allows access to the subconscious mind. Another easy way to foster mindfulness in kids is to teach them how to do walking mediation. The slow rhythmic movements help them quiet their minds. If your children walk to a bus stop each morning, have them do it mindfully and pay attention to what they hear, see, and feel as they walk. If you walk with them, you can practice, too, and say out loud the things you see, feel, and hear. The key is to walk with awareness and take in the experience of the outside world. It is amazing what you will notice.

A fun way for children to become aware of their breath is to have them lie down on their back and place a small toy on their belly. Tell them to take a deep breath in and see the toy rise, and as they breathe out, the toy will sink. Have them take several deep breaths while focusing on the toy's rising and falling. Another trick is to have them pretend their raised fingers are birthday candles. Ask them to inhale and blow each one out individually. Or they can make a bowl by cupping their hands together. Then encourage them to take a deep breath in and slowly breathe out filling up their bowl.

Once Tyler got a taste of meditation and its benefits, he started doing it on his own more and more. On a car ride to tae kwon do, Mike looked in the rearview mirror and thought Tyler had fallen asleep. Mike asked, "Hey buddy, you awake?" Tyler calmly opened his eyes and said in a matter-of-fact tone, "Yeah dad, I was just meditating." Sometimes Tyler sits under a tree in lotus pose at the bus stop to meditate while he waits for the bus to arrive. Tyler has even created his own meditation that he calls the "Shrinking Golden Balls." He imagines any negative thought or fear as a golden ball in his mind's eye then imagines it shrinking down until it disappears. This usually takes him a grand total of 30 seconds, but at age seven, he doesn't have too many negative thoughts. Kids naturally live in the present moment,

THE MIRACLE MORNING FOR PARENTS & FAMILIES

so they don't need to sit in silence for long periods of time to gain the benefits of meditation. Just exposing them to the idea and having them do simple mindfulness practices is more than enough. They will at least be aware that they have tools to manage stress as they grow and the demands on them become more intense.

Service

> S is for service. When we help others, it makes us feel good too.
>
> Lend a helping hand.
>
> Clean up your mess, feed the dog,
>
> or just get along.

Mahatma Gandhi said, "The best way to find yourself is to lose yourself in the service of others." Children today get a bad rap for being self-absorbed and lazy, but I don't think that is the case at all. I believe kids are not given the opportunity to serve. In the age of helicopter parenting, we are doing our kids a disservice when we don't allow them to do things for themselves and for others. New studies show that empathy and compassion are hardwired from birth. In one study, researchers entered a room with their arms full and dropped a clothespin. While straining to reach for it, the one-year-old participants would speedily come to the adults' rescue, sometimes even overcoming obstacles to help. If the researchers purposely threw the peg down, the children were much less likely to come to their aid. In another study with six-month-old babies, the young ones were shown stuffed animals, and one would be mean to another. When given the choice of which toy to play with, the child predominantly always chose the "nice" toy.

Other studies show that the reward centers of the brain light up when people use money to buy a gift for someone else. It simply feels good to be of service, so there is no need for any extra reward (except maybe a thank-you).

I believe you should expect your kids to do chores, but you should not pay them for the work. After all, mom and dad do chores around the house and receive no pay for it. Kids should be expected to pitch in too. Consider your child's age when assigning chores, but even a two-year-old can put their dirty laundry in a hamper and help put toys away in a toy box. Yes, it can be time-consuming to teach kids how to do chores, but if we don't, we rob our children of the good feelings they get from being helpful. It can be really frustrating when you're trying to get out the door in the morning and your toddler insists on putting on her own shoes, but in the long run, it will make your life easier. If you invest the time when they are young, they will learn to tackle bigger challenges and problems as they grow. By the time they are teenagers they can choose to legally get a job to take on even more responsibility.

There are many ways you can show your children how to be of service to others. Here are a few:

- Model small acts of kindness, including smiling at someone, giving a compliment, or donating toys.

- Encourage your kids to brainstorm ideas on how they can help in your community.

- Help them set up a lemonade stand to raise money for a charity they feel passionate about.

- Volunteer together for a local nonprofit organization.

- Use VolunteerMatch.com to find opportunities in your area that may be open to families or children.

Tyler and I have volunteered to clean up local parks, to organize donations and shred papers for a homeless shelter, and to help clean shoes for Cradles to Crayons. Tyler supported our local hospital through his tae kwon do school and asked for donations in our neighborhood. With his cub scout pack, he has collected canned goods for the less fortunate and volunteered time at a local nursing home to do arts and crafts with the elderly residents. Mike's GoBundance Mastermind group in partnership with the non-profit 1Life Fully Lived (1LifeFullyLived.org) organizes a turkey drive each year for Thanksgiving, and the kids help package the meals and hand them out to less fortunate families. In the first year, 2014, they fed 300 families, and the next year they fed 1,000 families. If you would like to support the cause, please visit TurkeyBundance.org (One hundred percent of your donations go to the meals).

There are so many ways to get your kids involved in service, but the best way (as with most things) is to model it yourself. If we want to raise compassionate kids, it starts with us.

Other Tips and Tricks

As we have introduced our kids to the Miracle Morning and have been practicing it as a family, we have learned what works for us. Here are some tips and tricks from the trenches.

- **Get up at least 30 minutes before your kids do.** Start your Miracle Morning with whatever is most important or the hardest to do with your kids awake. Hal recommends going deep (and I agree) with whichever of the Life S.A.V.E.R.S. gives you the most bang for your buck if you don't have time to do them all.

- **Forgive yourself if you need to skip a day or modify your Miracle Morning.** You may have an ideal practice in mind, but if one night your child wakes up in the middle of the night because they are scared, have to pee, are sick, or for whatever reason, it's okay (I believe better) to modify your practice. Some parents break up the Life S.A.V.E.R.S. and do them throughout the day until they can get on a consistent schedule. Hal's good friend and business partner Jon Berghoff explained to us that the best method for goal setting is the one you will actually use. That goes for your Miracle Morning practice too.

- **Combine Life S.A.V.E.R.S. or C.H.A.R.M.S.** Our kids love doing their affirmations while jumping on a trampoline or doing other exercises. They can also combine creativity and health. For creativity, I have them make up their own exercises. Health and service can be combined if their service is to cook the family breakfast or pack a healthy lunch for a sibling. Meditation and health can be combined if they do a walking meditation or practice yoga. They could combine reading and service by reading to a younger sibling as well. The possibilities are endless!

- **Make their C.H.A.R.M.S. into a game.** We created a C.H.A.R.M.S. die, so when the kids are having a hard time choosing which one to do first, all they have to do is roll the die, and it makes the decision for them. Go to www-MiracleMorning.com/parents to get your free download of the paper C.H.A.R.M.S. die to print at home (I suggest using card stock to make it sturdier). Also on that website is a C.H.A.R.M.S. tracker, so your kids can keep track of their C.H.A.R.M.S. on their own. Tyler gets great joy checking off his C.H.A.R.M.S. each morning. I laminated ours so the kids can use dry erase markers and reuse it each week.

- **Help your kids get organized.** Tyler and Ember each have their own Miracle Morning box where they keep everything they need (I used a standard size photo box that you can get at any craft store). In the box, they have the C.H.A.R.M.S. die, their homemade affirmation book, a book of their choosing to read, something to write with, a blank journal for creativity, and a one-minute sand timer. The timer can be used for several of the C.H.A.R.M.S. We often use it for health. We will do an exercise until the sand runs out then flip it and do it again. You can also use the timer itself as a meditation practice. Have the kids focus on the falling sand. Sometimes if the kids are resistant to creativity, I tell them to do it for one minute and start the timer, and by the time the sand is gone, they are absorbed in their activity. If you're more high-tech, timer apps can be used as well, Lickety Split is one we've used.

Flexibility Is Essential

It's important to have flexibility with your Miracle Morning when you have young lives that need your loving attention in the morning, but it doesn't end there. Flexibility also means going with the flow in life and listening to that still quiet voice that we all have inside us. Even when you do get your full Miracle Morning in first thing after waking, it's great to check back in with yourself throughout the day to make sure you are still on track. Mike and I like to set an intention for our day during our Miracle Morning, and occasionally we check in to see if we are still living that intention later on.

In our brains, neurons that fire together wire together. This is why your three-year-old always wants to sit at the same table at a restaurant (and freaks out if someone else is sitting at *your* table). If you take your child out for ice cream after their first soccer game, they will expect it after each game. This is how habits are created, which can save us a great deal of time in the long run. Using this principle, you can start to associate actions you do every day with checking back in with yourself. For example, I wash the dishes every day (sometimes multiple times per day). Every time I'm at the sink, the warm water on my hands reminds me to think about the things for which I'm grateful. As I clean the food off the dishes, I imagine that my fears, doubts, and worries go down the drain with the water. Then when I turn on the garbage disposal, I imagine those negative thoughts being fully eliminated from my mind. We can create rituals throughout our day without any added effort by being mindful and playful. And we can teach our kids to do this too.

Another part of being flexible is choosing your battles with your kids. Our good friend and author of the *Power of Identity*, Rock Thomas, says, "He who is most flexible wins." I agree with him, especially when it comes to battles with the kids. Young children are not typically very flexible. When they have their mind set on something, it can be very difficult to get them to change course. Often it's better to change your approach than to get into a power struggle with your child.

Ember is named appropriately. Before she was even a thought, an intuitive friend told us she would be a girl and a "spitfire." We chose her name loosely on this information, and she is certainly a girl who knows what she wants! She is not very fond of being told no, so we have learned to be flexible and playful with her, finding alternative ways to communicate.

In martial arts, they teach you to use your opponent's energy against them. This is more effective than resisting or fighting back. When we remove the struggle during conflict, we can go with the flow. We can allow our children's energy to carry them through the issue without being in the center of the conflict. Sometimes it is our resistance that perpetuates the conflict itself. So if you don't give your child something to push against, the resistance will dissipate. Imagine two hands pushing against each other; when one hand is removed the other is free to move forward unencumbered.

I've found that when we make our expectations clear as parents, it helps remind the children that we are in charge. For example, in our house the kids are allowed only two hours of screen time per day. They get to choose when they enjoy that time (as long as they have completed their Life C.H.A.R.M.S.) and on which device, but once the two hours is up, it's up. They don't like it when they are told screen time is over for the day, but they also know that they aren't going to get any more, so they don't fight it. When we first put this rule in place, there was massive resistance from the kids, but after a few weeks of our being absolutely clear about the limit, they stopped fighting us. We were no longer the bad guys. It had simply become the new normal.

Final Thoughts on Playfulness

Play is such an important outlet for stress for both kids and parents. When we play together, we truly connect with each other and can be silly and vulnerable. Home is the best place to foster play. It's also a fun way to start the day. Creating the C.H.A.R.M.S. with Tyler has been one of the biggest parenting wins I've had.

I encourage you to have fun with your Miracle Morning routine, to talk to your kids about the changes you're making, and allow them the gift of their own practice. The beauty of the Miracle Morning is that it's not one size fits all. Play with it and find out what works for you and your family.

Success Stories

Here is what some other parents have done to be flexible with their Miracle Morning and their young people.

Sarah Dena from the United Kingdom said this: "After a weekend away from the Miracle Morning practice (planned and by choice), I am grateful to be back again! This morning my eldest daughter woke early ... just after my 5:00 a.m. alarm. She decided to read in her room, but it didn't last. Soon she was by my side following my yoga practice. She listened to my affirmations. Visualizations seemed to bore her, so she went to her playroom and turned on her music player

... acting out the scenes to Mamma Mia. I was grateful. Her appearance during 'my time,' distracted and frustrated me, but I let it go and recommitted to my morning practice. The last line I read was 'Gratitude, always' (from Elizabeth Gilbert's *Big Magic*). As I went to the playroom, I stopped and listened. She was using the microphone to speak out her own version of affirmations! I left her to be in that moment. It was beautiful!"

Elana Carr said, "My daughter is three, and usually she'll sleep until around 8:00 a.m., so I get up around 5:00 a.m. On days that she's up, we do things together. We pray together, say affirmations together, and I ask her questions about what she wants when we . . . (whatever my visualization is about). While she draws I write, while she's relaxing I'll read, and then we'll jump around together to get the blood flowing. It may take longer than an hour to do, but it gets it done."

Vica Hickmann said, "When I first tried to do the Miracle Morning, my little one (she's three) started getting up earlier and earlier, and I gave up. Then I got an accountability partner, and we started the 30-day challenge. I have been doing everything inside my bedroom, so my daughter doesn't wake up. It has been working. I leave things ready, and I use my mobile for mediation, exercise (7 Minute Workout app), and affirmations. We're also using *May Cause Miracles: A 40-Day Guidebook of Subtle Shifts for Radical Change and Unlimited Happiness*, by Gabby Bernstein."

I commend these awesome parents because they are taking action and being great role models for their kids!

PARENTING PROFILE

Ursula Elrod

Ursula is a stay-at-home mom with two children, ages seven and four. She has been happily married to Hal Elrod, the author of *The Miracle Morning*, for seven years.

Parenting Philosophy

I want to raise children who don't need to recover from their childhood. Parenting with purpose is making sure you're raising people who don't need therapy and who don't carry issues into their own parenting down the road.

Sharing the Miracle Morning with the kids. My daughter loves the exercise part because she loves doing yoga, and my son loves doing seven-minute workout with Hal. He asks for it: "Dad, let's do seven-minute workout." It's so great.

Affirmation tips for kids. Some friends of ours showed us the Affirmation Alligator. They made an alligator out of an old shoebox and a tissue box. Every morning, the kids get to reach their hands into the mouth of the alligator and pull out an affirmation for the day. Can be found here: http://tinyurl.com/hnj7lsx.

Best Parenting Tips

Discipline can be playful. I don't have a traditional out-of-the-house career. My career is my children right now. When I do the Miracle Morning, I become more present and aware of how I need to be. I handle things more playfully, even discipline. One of the books I read says kids can release stress in two ways—crying or laughter. Typically, children will cry because of the parent. The parent loses their temper, and so the children cry. When something gets frustrating, it's either, "Okay, they're going to cry, or they're going to laugh." I try to make my children laugh. I try to ask myself, how can I show them that life isn't that big a deal, and we don't need to get that stressed out about it?

Free yourself from outdated parenting styles. I think we're all guilty of falling into our own parenting habits because of how we were parented. Because of the Miracle Morning, I'm discovering that my own parenting style can be different from the way I was raised. I'm finding ways to become a better parent and not just go through the motions of parenting. There are so many parents I see on Facebook who joke, "Oh, if my kids weren't cute, I'd spank them." It's sad that we joke about losing patience with our kids when really, we need to be there for our children because they're only little for so long.

It's okay to let our children struggle. I don't think we're doing any service to our children by sheltering them and taking care of everything. Let them get hurt. Let them struggle a little. Like the saying, "Just when the caterpillar thought the world was over, he became a beautiful butterfly." To become that butterfly, he had to struggle. Your kids will feel so much more accomplished, and they'll be willing to try more new things knowing that they can do it.

Celebrate their accomplishments, however small. When children do something, when they achieve something new, be sure to acknowledge it. When my daughter started riding her bike without training wheels, she was so excited. She couldn't wait until Hal came home to show him and tell him all about it. When my son learned how to swim, he could not wait to show Hal. Those accomplishments are so big for them in their young lives that you have to let them feel that joy.

Take care of your marriage. Here's the thing: you're going to love your kids unconditionally, no matter what. Your spouse on the other hand, you've got to work at that relationship, especially when kids come along because it becomes stressful. Life becomes hectic with after-school activities and vacations and in-laws and everything.

Great Parenting Resources

One of the books I recommend is *Screamfree Parenting: The Revolutionary Approach to Raising Your Kids by Keeping Your Cool* by Hal Edward Runkel. I'd also recommend *The Five Love Languages of Children* by Gary Chapman and Ross Campbell. It's a guide for how to make them feel loved. Everyone hears the message of love differently, whether it's from receiving gifts or words of affirmation, whatever. It helps you to learn that.

Parenting Success Story

We did a hybrid homeschool program with our daughter for kindergarten. This last week has been a bit stressful. She had to finish all of her schoolwork for kindergarten graduation. My son, being an amazing little brother says, "It's okay, I'll do my homework with you." I got out a preschool book for him to work on. They had the best time laughing and hanging out with each other and doing their homework, kidding and racing. "Who can do their homework faster?" The whole time she was stressed out, he was just there saying, "I'll do it with you."

Final Word

When you really put good in, you get so much good out. It's just amazing to see how strong you can build your family when you take the time and you make the effort to become a better parent.

PARENTING PROFILE

Jon Berghoff

Jon began his career as a distributor for Cutco Cutlery, achieving the top spot in sales in his first year. For more than a decade now, Jon has uncovered, tested, and taught sales and influence strategies. Jon's interactive trainings have reached over 75,000 live students internationally, and he has conducted over 3,500 private coaching calls with clients from more than 100 professions and trades.

Jon is married with three kids, ages six, four, and two.

Parenting Philosophy

Recognize that your kids are always learning from you. Every single thing I do is a form of training for my kids. I used to sit down with my kids and give them little talks. Short, three- to five-minute life lessons. The first 100 times I did that, I kept thinking, *Why aren't they responding in some profound way?* Well, a five-year-old just might not be capable of externalizing a response yet. I've come to realize that, regardless of how they respond, it's sinking in. If I ask my son something deep and profound, and I want a profound answer, 99 times out of 100, he responds by talking about superheroes. But what happens next is that, all of a sudden, I do get a profound response. I'm reminded that the other 99 times the lesson is still sinking in.

Best Parenting Tips

Spend time with your kids. It's not about the quantity; it's about the quality. That doesn't mean that the quality is always where I would like it to be, but that is something that I think about.

Make it tactical. I ask myself all the time, how can I involve my kids in things where it would be easy not to involve them? For example, exercise. I've realized I could make an excuse, or I could involve them in my exercise routine. If I put them in a stroller and add weights underneath, I can work out intensely, and my kids don't even realize that's what I'm doing. They think we're running through the woods on our way to the playground.

Be willing to learn from your children. Having kids has given me a very rich sense of meaning that my life didn't have before. My kids have taught me to have a certain amount of humility around the way I think the world should be.

Pay attention. I think there's probably a lot of parents that are sleepwalking, just trying to make it through the day. They don't realize that their kids are reflecting back to them both their greatest weaknesses and greatest strengths. What a great learning opportunity. If you pay attention, you can use the information to become a better person, and a better parent.

Parenting Success Story

My son didn't seem to like soccer, a sport I was really good at. That was tough for me. But I had to realize that kids get engaged at their own individual unique pace. They get interested. It's not something that we can control. My wife and I decided that we're going to expose our kids to anything they want to be exposed to, no matter what we think of it.

We changed our way of thinking to focus on the child rather than ourselves. So now we ask, what are they enjoying, and what are they good at? This helped us stop putting them in environments that they don't want to be in and to find the ones they want to be in.

Final Word

Remember the impermanence of everything. My daughter is only going to be four once. It's so easy for me to see everything that's frustrating and say to myself, I can't wait until she's eight. I try to remind myself that there are things about this age that I'm never going to experience again. Whether it's a certain innocence or a certain playfulness, every stage has something that's beautiful about it. If we're constantly waiting until they get through the current phase, then we're unconsciously disengaging. Reconnect to what's great about the chapter they're in. Appreciate it and let them know.

— 9 —
EXCEPTIONAL PARENTING SKILL #3:
PERSPECTIVE

For what you see and hear depends a good deal on where you are standing: it also depends on what sort of person you are.
— C.S. Lewis, British novelist and poet, best known for *The Chronicles of Narnia*

I'm going to share with you an experience I recently had with my daughter. It started like this:

"I want to wear my party dress!"

"But Ember, we're going snow skiing."

"I don't care! I just want to wear my party dress!"

Why is it so hard to understand our young children's reasoning? And what strategies can we use to help effective communication take place? I've got some interesting information for you that might help you better handle a meltdown next time you encounter one. And it all has to do with perspective.

As adults, we often have trouble seeing the world as our child does. The reason for this is that we literally see things differently. The word perspective has a Latin root meaning "to look through, to perceive."

Your perspective is essentially the way you see the world. Unless your kids are in their mid-twenties or older, their brains are not yet fully developed, and as a result, they have a different perspective than we do as adults. For us to see things the way they do, it's helpful to know a little about how the brain works.

In the book *The Whole-Brain Child* the authors Daniel J. Siegel, MD, and Tina Payne Bryson, PhD, explain the brain in basic terms using the analogy of a house. The "downstairs brain" is made up of the brainstem and the limbic region that control the involuntary functions of the body, like your heartbeat and breathing, your reactions, and strong emotions. The "upstairs brain" consists of the prefrontal cortex where the higher functions of thinking, planning, and imagining take place.

The authors elaborate on their analogy this way:

Even though we will want to help build this metaphorical staircase in our child's brain, there are two important reasons to maintain realistic expectations when it comes to integration. The first is developmental: while the downstairs brain is well developed even at birth, the upstairs brain isn't fully mature until a person reaches their mid-twenties. In fact, it's one of the last parts of the brain to develop. The upstairs brain remains under massive construction for the first few years of life, then during the teen years undergoes an extensive remodel that lasts into adulthood.

This reminds me of the movie *Inside Out*. The main character, Riley, has five emotions in headquarters (her brain): Joy, Sadness, Fear, Anger and Disgust. She also has four "Islands of Personality," that make her who she is as an individual. Riley was born with Joy, and the other four emotions show up very soon after (the downstairs brain), and the "Islands of Personality" develop in the first few years of life (the beginnings of the upstairs brain). Riley goes through a hard time in her life because she moves across the country with her family. She loses Joy and Sadness along with all her Islands of Personality. By the end of the movie, Riley (now age 12) gets an upgraded console (which controls her emotions) and develops all new Islands or Personality. Around puberty, we all had a major construction project going on in our upstairs brains.

Even teenagers, who seem so grown up on the outside, do not have the brainpower or the experience that we do as adults. Teens use their prefrontal cortex to make decisions regarding risk and painstakingly weigh their options (sometimes carefully, other times foolishly), taking twice as long to decide as compared to adults. Because we adults have made so many decisions in our lifetimes, we delegate this task to another part of the brain, so that these decisions become almost automatic. If you asked an adult to make a decision that involves substantial risk or potential bodily harm, they would most likely say no quickly. Teens, in contrast, are motivated by possible rewards and often will ignore the potentially dangerous consequences. Even though teens will actually slow down and use the reasoning part of their brain to make the choice, they are still more likely to say yes than adults.

The other main reason we need to keep realistic expectations when it comes to our kids' brains has to do with one particular part of the downstairs brain, the amygdala. The authors describe the amygdala like a baby gate that can trap us downstairs. For the purposes of sticking with the house theme, I'd say it's like the security system. When the security system starts blaring, it doesn't matter what had been going on, everyone jumps up and springs into action without thinking. This is what the amygdala does. It makes the body go into action without thinking. The amygdala is where our fight, flight, or freeze response comes from. Adults can also go into reaction mode, but we have a fully functioning prefrontal cortex to help us get back to logical thinking. After the initial shock when the security system goes off, we can calmly go to the keypad and punch in the code to bring order back to the house. For children, when the security system goes off, they may not know the code. They may need our help to turn it off and settle their nervous systems.

Not only are our children's brains still developing, but there's a part of their brain that can fully stop the upstairs brain from functioning at all. Knowing this, it makes sense that Ember can't be reasoned with when she wants to wear a party dress to go skiing. I can tell her all the logical reasons her desire doesn't make sense, but her security system is blaring in her ear, and she can't hear me.

All is not lost. There are techniques for helping children turn off the security systems. They work by engaging the child's higher brain function. Next time your child has a meltdown, try these techniques:

- **Physical touch**: To turn off the security system at home, you have to physically enter a number into a keypad. Touch is also surprisingly effective to calm down human beings. Physically holding your child's hand, holding her in your arms, or taking a walk with her can sometimes be just what she needs to turn off the alarm so she can think again.

- **Problem Solving**: Asking questions that get children thinking is another strategy. When there is a conflict in progress, we can ask them for solutions. Children often do not like being told what to do, so instead of giving them commands, we can include their input to get an easier buy-in.

- **Presenting Options**: Another great thing to do (especially with young ones) is to give them some options to choose from. This gives them a sense of independence without overwhelming them.

- **Using humor:** A technique to decrease conflict is to engage your child's sense of humor. If you can lighten the mood by making them laugh, it will help them move away from feeling threatened to a calmer state of mind. One thing we do quite often when our kids are grumpy is to say, "You better not smile" which works like a charm.

I know you're wondering how I handled the actual situation when Ember was upset about the party dress. Here's what I did. I picked her up and held her close and spun her around, which made her smile. Once she calmed down, I asked, "Have you ever seen someone skiing in a party dress?" Ember replied, "Yes, in my magazine." She was referring to her *High Five*™ magazine. One puzzle in the magazine is called "That's Silly!" and it had a snow scene where she thought she saw someone skiing with a party dress on. I got the magazine and asked Ember to show me. We flipped to the page and saw a lot of funny things, but no one skiing in a party dress. I asked her to point out some things that were silly on the page. Ember saw people sunbathing in bathing suits in the snow, a cat driving a car, a gingerbread house and squirrels playing tic-tac-toe. We laughed at all the goofy things we saw. Then I asked her, "Do you think skiing in a party dress is silly too?" She answered yes with a laugh. At that point, we could easily pick out the appropriate clothing and move on with the day. Yes, this did take some time, but the alternative would have surely ended in yelling, tears, and hurt feelings on both sides.

I talked a little about mirror neurons and their power for visualizations for the Life S.A.V.E.R.S., but they are also very powerful for our children's brain development. In *The Whole-Brain Child*, Siegel and Bryson explain it:

As children develop, their brains "mirror" their parent's brain. In other words, the parent's own growth and development, or lack of those, impact the child's brain. As parents become more aware and emotionally healthy, their children reap the rewards and move toward health as well. That means that integrating and cultivating your own brain is one of the most loving and generous gifts you can give your child.

It's a healthy perspective to want to develop your brain. I believe the best way to work on your personal development is by committing to the Miracle Morning. If you are ready to commit, you can visit www.TMMBook.com and start your 30-day challenge today!

Teaching Empathy to Your Children

In the last chapter, I revealed research that showed empathy and compassion are inborn, and recent research has shown that empathy is a skill that can be taught as well. The Making Caring Common Project at the Harvard Graduate School of Education is an organization dedicated to helping educators, parents, and communities raise children who are caring, responsible to their communities, and committed to justice. Scientists there point out that, while empathy begins with the ability to walk in another's shoes, it is more than just that. After all, politicians, actors and marketers are often adept at putting themselves in someone else's shoes, but they may not care about others. So the definition of empathy also includes compassion.

How can parents cultivate empathy in their kids? Richard Weissbourd and Stephanie Jones from the Making Caring Common Project recommend the following five techniques:

1. Empathize with your child and model empathy for others.

Because children learn empathy both from watching us and from experiencing our empathy for them, modeling the behavior is very important. Empathizing with our children is a way to form trusting, secure attachments with them, which inspires them to emulate us. You can show your child empathy by tuning in to their physical and emotional needs, respecting their individual personalities, showing an interest in their lives, and guiding them toward activities that reflect who they are.

2. Set high ethical expectations and make caring for others a priority.

To help children learn to value others' perspectives and show compassion for them, it's crucial that they hear from you that caring about others is important and that other people's feelings are just as important as their own. Children need to understand that the world doesn't revolve around them. So teach your kids to turn off the TV and help around the house, be polite even when they are in a bad mood, and give others a chance to talk during a discussion.

3. Provide opportunities for children to practice empathy.

Children may be born with the capacity for empathy, but it is a skill that should be nurtured throughout their lives. Empathy requires practice and guidance. When you make a practice of regularly considering other people's perspectives and circumstances, this helps make empathy a natural reflex and, through trial and error, helps children get better at it.

4. Expand your child's circle of concern.

It's easy to have empathy for our family members and close friends. And it's human nature to have empathy for people who are like us in some way. But the real issue is whether children (and adults) have empathy outside that circle. So it's important to model appreciation for many types of people. We can help our children to understand and care about people who are different from them and who may be facing challenges very different from their own challenges. Encourage children to consider the feelings of those who may be vulnerable, such as a child experiencing some family trouble or an unpopular child. Give them simple ideas for taking action, like comforting a classmate who has been teased.

5. Help children develop self-control and manage feelings effectively.

It's possible that empathy can be blocked by some feeling or image strong enough to overwhelm the ability to care about others. Anger, shame, envy, or other negative feelings can have this effect. So it's important to help children manage these negative feelings as well as stereotypes and prejudices about others so that they can let their empathy come out.

When you take the time to teach your children empathy, you are doing a lot to help them become caring, compassionate adults who will do good in the world. And you decrease the amount of self-centeredness as well. As Daniel Goleman put it in *Social Intelligence: The New Science of Human Relationships*, "Self-absorption in all its forms kills empathy, let alone compassion. When we focus on ourselves, our world contracts as our problems and preoccupations loom large. But when we focus on others, our world expands. Our own problems drift to the periphery of the mind and so seem smaller, and we increase our capacity for connection—or compassionate action."

Perfection Doesn't Exist

One of the biggest burdens parents carry is the pressure to be perfect. Our children depend on us for everything. With so much at stake, most parents want to do everything right. They tend to beat themselves up over every mistake.

Let me relieve you of that burden right here and now: There is no such thing as a perfect parent. It's an impossible goal and chasing it only leads to negativity. We are all only human. We do the best we can with the information we have at the time. Hal says, "Give up being perfect for being authentic." This rings so true for me as a parent. Our children want us to be happy. The best thing we can do for them is to focus on becoming the best version of ourselves that we can be. Mike and I are certainly not perfect parents, but we are committed to learning new things and open to new approaches and to allowing our kids to empower us to become better parents. We don't get it right 100 percent of the time, so don't feel like you are failing if you don't implement everything in this book.

It's a tall order to be a person you want your child to look up to and emulate, but that's what parenting is all about. It's about showing our kids that we are not perfect and demonstrating how to get past the struggles of everyday life. It's about being vulnerable and authentic with them. As parents we don't have to know all the answers, but we should be willing to seek them out. As Brené Brown, PhD, says, "It's actually our ability to embrace imperfection that will help us teach our children to have the courage to be authentic, the compassion to love themselves and others, and the sense of connection that gives true purpose and meaning to life."

Perfectionism Is Just Another Form of Fear

Perfection seems like the highest calling, but it actually leads to inaction and a lack of creativity. When we are afraid of making mistakes or looking like we're not perfect, we spend so much time and energy on keeping up the act that we don't have the time or energy to actually live the life of our dreams. Perfection is also relative. Your idea of perfect parenting may be in complete opposition to another's idea. I've found that it's much better to be clear about your family's values and create your ideal life from there. No matter where you are in your life right now, change is coming. Kids grow up, cars break down, people make mistakes, things go wrong, but they also turn out better than you ever could have expected. Focus on what you do want in life, and you'll be surprised at how much of it shows up.

Leave the goal of perfection behind and focus on progress instead. The one minute of meditation you do is better than zero minutes. The sushi takeout eaten together as a family is better than the four course organic meal you made from scratch that left you no time to enjoy dinner together. The movie you watch with your spouse after the kids go to sleep is better than the dinner out on the town you can't make because the babysitter cancelled last minute. When we can be comfortable with our mistakes and share that comfort with our kids, they will adopt the same mindset.

Our friend, author Rock Thomas, suggests asking yourself, What's great about this? It may not be what you had in mind, but if you can take the perspective that whatever is happening is already perfect, your life will be happier. Embrace what is and make the best of it. As Hal would say, you can't change it, so focus on moving on and enjoying whatever is great about it!

Gratitude

Our brains are literally wired for bad news. Information about what's wrong is always available to us. You can choose to focus on that, or you can look for what's right in the world. Gratitude is one of the best perspectives that we can form. When we focus on what's working, the progress we've made, and the things we did get right, it's amazing how our confidence and energy soar. Focusing on the opposite, by obsessing over the mistakes you made, reliving the past, or beating yourself up for things you can't change, will leave you feeling empty and alone. A perspective shift from destructive thoughts to gratitude can be a gateway to finding the solutions that will actually move you forward from any sticky situation. Scientists have found that the magic ratio is five to one. As long as we experience positivity five times more than negativity, we can remain grateful. The exercise of simply writing down a few things you are grateful for daily can turn your world upside down, or in this case, right side up!

Shifting Perspective on the Past

Can you change the past? No, but you can change your perspective. Our past is simply our memory of what happened. It's just one possible perspective. If something happened in the past, which it surely did, then the ways in which you grow from that past experience will change what actually happened. You can choose the meaning of your experiences and create new meaning in the future by choosing new actions. So if you want to change the past, then allow it to empower you today. Simply choose new meaning for what happened and allow that to inspire new action today then you will have effectively shifted the past.

People with a growth mindset believe intelligence comes from effort, while those with a fixed mindset believe they are born with a fixed amount of intelligence that cannot be changed. Students with a growth mindset outperform their peers with a fixed mindset. We can help foster a growth mindset in our kids by the way we praise them. For example, when your child brings home a good grade, congratulate them on how hard they worked instead of for how smart they are. When your child scores a goal in a soccer game, instead of saying, "You're a natural," remind them how focused they were at practice. On the flip side, if your child did poorly in the game, instead of saying, "You just aren't cut out for soccer," encourage them to work harder at the next opportunity. You can help them brainstorm ways to improve. They could add a soccer visualization meditation to their

Miracle Morning or some affirmations about soccer. The idea is to get your kids to realize they have the power to change the outcome by the work they put in.

In her book, *The Gift of Failure*, Jessica Lahey explains what our children need from us:

> *As they progress from team to team, and league to league, or give up sports completely, children rely on parents to anchor their family team and provide the kind of unwavering support that can help them through their most humiliating and humbling failures. In those moments, they need us to remind them that as long as they show up on the field and do their very best, in sports or anywhere else, we will keep our end of the bargain and show up on the sidelines to cheer them on.*

As a former division 1 field hockey player, I can attest that my parents' support on the sidelines meant the world to my teammates and me. After a hard fought game, win or lose, to be congratulated or comforted by our home team made it worth all the effort we'd put in.

Our Children as Teachers

As a life-long learner with a growth mindset, I believe I can grow and learn from any experience and through any teacher, including my children. When I view my children as my teachers, I can release a lot of struggle. Kids are naturally more present than adults. They are more playful, more observant and more curious. If you pay attention to your child's observations about you, you will see things from a revealing perspective. Our children reflect back to us both our strengths and our weaknesses.

One afternoon while driving Tyler to soccer practice, I looked at the passenger seat and saw the tax bills sitting there. I had totally forgotten to take them to the post office that morning, and of course it was the last day to submit them without a penalty. Upon noticing them, my "security system" starting blaring, and I told the kids we'd have to reroute and miss soccer that day. Tyler in his wisdom calmly asked questions, which activated my "upstairs brain," and we began problem solving. Together we came up with the plan for me to drop him at soccer practice (he reminded me that I didn't have to stay), drive to the post office, and get back in time to pick him up.

At the post office, the line was very long and most people were there for the same reason, so it was quite a grumpy scene, except for Ember. She was content to look at the cards and even started twirling in her princess skirt and playing peekaboo with the gentleman behind us, making everyone smile.

That day Tyler mirrored my typical patience and calmness to me when I needed it most, and Ember reminded me to enjoy each moment in life, even if it's waiting in line to pay your taxes!

Here's another example: When Mike and Tyler had their first Family Board Meeting, they were in the garage working on their remote control cars when Mike observed Tyler and was overcome with appreciation for him. Mike told Tyler that he was proud of him and was so grateful that he had come here to teach him about love and soften his heart. He let Tyler know how much he loved to watch him playing in his element in the workshop. Tyler climbed up on the step stool that was next to them, becoming taller than Mike, and kissed him on his forehead like a father would do to his son. That day in the garage, a role reversal had taken place. Tyler became Mike's teacher, and Mike had become Tyler's willing student.

When we allow our kids the opportunity to teach us something, we often learn so much more and they feel valued and appreciated in a whole new way. Mike acknowledged Tyler not only as a child and student, but also as a teacher. It was one of his most proud and beautiful moments as a father.

By being open to it, Mike and I have learned patience, acceptance, understanding, gratitude, love, purpose, legacy, passion, the cycle of life, and more from our kids. We believe that this is a healthy perspective and one that allows us to connect at a deeper level. Expressing appreciation has become a daily practice in our house. During our morning, we do a family hug and will share our gratitude with each other. This is such a nice way to start the day, and it brings us closer together as a family.

The last perspective that brings everything together is cultivating the view that we are all on our own unique journey. We are all here to live out our purpose. As Kahlil Gibran says in his beautiful poem "On Children,"

Your children are not your children.

They are the sons and daughters of Life's longing for itself.

They come through you but not from you,

And though they are with you yet they belong not to you.

Parenting and the Hero's Journey

We recently had the privilege of hearing Pat Solomon speak about his experience making the film *Finding Joe* about the renowned American comparative mythologist Joseph Campbell. Campbell spent his career studying and analyzing myths from many cultures, and observed that these stories contained many common elements, which he related to our human journey by creating a framework called, the Hero's Journey. It's this very concept that is drives humanity's obsession for classic hero stories, such as *Star Wars*, *The Lord of the Rings*, and *Rocky*. We are fascinated by the hero's or heroine's plight in these stories, and we are inspired and reminded to become the hero of our own life story. We all root for the hero because, in the end, we are one and the same.

In his talk, Solomon added the idea that we all play different characters throughout our lives and are actually on many journeys simultaneously. For example, you may be early in your journey as a parent but further along in your journey as a businessperson. Or your journey as the parent of an infant may be ending as your journey as the parent of a toddler is just beginning. Each new phase brings a new set of challenges and joys. And each new child brings a unique set of strengths and opportunities for growth.

The Hero's Journey offers some great perspectives on parenting. It has three phases: Departure, Initiation, and Return.

Departure

We all start in our ordinary world. Here we may feel stuck or experience a lack of awareness; we simply don't know what we don't know yet. We then experience a call to adventure. This can be something simple like the urge to follow a butterfly into the forest or something big like the desire to write a book. Our first reaction to the call is often resistance. We don't want to leave our comfort zone. We may feel stuck, but the unknown alternative is scarier, so we stay put. Next we meet a mentor. A mentor can come in many forms. It could be a person, like a teacher or coach, but it could also be a book or an idea.

Initiation

The first stage in Initiation is Crossing the Threshold. Once a commitment is made to the call, there is no returning to your ordinary world. This step can come on purpose (you quit your job to pursue your passion) or it can be thrust upon you (you're fired), but either way, there is no turning back. When you have a child, you cross a major threshold. We can embrace the journey with its tests, allies, and enemies, or we can resist them, but we can't go back.

The next step is the Approach. This is a time when we approach the metaphoric treasure. In parenting this may be when our kids go off to college or take over the family business, get married or become parents of their own. You have to define your own treasure as a parent. Don't forget to celebrate the small victories on the way to the big treasure. For us, the ultimate treasure is to have children who know their purpose on this Earth and love it every day, but to get there you have to celebrate their small victories (taking their first steps, learning to tie their shoes, riding a bike independently, etc.) and be there to pick them up when they fail (the first F on a test, first time they are called a name, falling off their bike, etc.).

After the Approach comes the Ordeal, also called Death and Rebirth. Here we lose a part of ourselves to grow into something or someone new. This happens many times in our parenting journey and includes everything from when your child rides the school bus for the first time to when you help them move into their college dorm room. An old part of us dies to create space for a new and improved version of ourselves. Before we can seize our treasure, we have to slay our dragons, which means facing our fears. When we do this, we find a sense of courage that was not there before.

After the Ordeal comes the Reward or "Seizing the Sword." Once a parent, you'll always be a parent to your children, and on that journey, you will be rewarded many times. Once your children learn to talk they will say, "I love you." When they learn to tie their shoes, you will be rewarded with extra minutes in the morning. When they learn to drive, you will be rewarded by not having to be their chauffeur. Each time they gain independence, you gain time to focus on something else.

This is not the end of the journey. Next is the Road Back. Once the treasure is found, the hero brings it home to share with the village.

Return

During the return stage a resurrection takes place. In the Ordeal, you lose a little of yourself in order to grow, but in this stage, you become a whole new person from the journey you've experienced. The last step in the journey is called Returning with the Elixir, and this is basically sharing the story of your adventure or, as I like to see it, leaving a legacy. After this stage, your journey may start over with a new ordinary world or, if it was your final journey, perhaps only the story will live on.

THE HERO'S JOURNEY

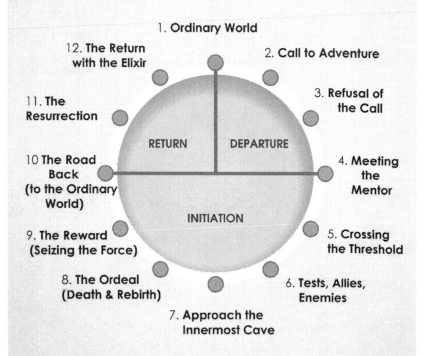

1. Ordinary World

12. The Return
with the Elixir

2. Call to Adventure

11. The
Resurrection

3. Refusal of
the Call

RETURN   DEPARTURE

10 The Road
Back
(to the Ordinary
World)

4. Meeting
the
Mentor

INITIATION

9. The Reward
(Seizing the Force)

5. Crossing
the Threshold

8. The Ordeal
(Death & Rebirth)

6. Tests, Allies,
Enemies

7. Approach the
Innermost Cave

Applying the Hero's Journey to Parenting

The Hero's Journey concept allows us to focus on the fact that we go on many journeys in life and that life itself is a journey. Using a real-world example of epic proportions, let me apply the Hero's Journey to potty training. Ember and I recently went on that journey together! At the beginning, our ordinary world was one of diapers and diaper bags with a clean set of clothes and wipes. The Call to Adventure was my goal of helping Ember to learn to use the potty. The Refusal of the Call was Ember's full-out tantrums and the little voice inside me that said, "Maybe it's too early. Wouldn't it be easier to just wait?" The meeting of the Mentor for me was the knowledge that, for Ember to participate in ski lessons, she had to be potty trained. Ember was very excited to learn to ski so she could come with Mom and Dad on the mountain and be like her big brother. This was her motivation to get over the fear of the unknown.

Crossing the Threshold happened when we got rid of the diapers and purchased new big girl underpants. Next came the Tests: reminding her to go before we left the house, always knowing where the closest bathroom was, and, of course, the accidents. Our Allies were other parents going through the same process as well as Ember's preschool teachers. The Enemy was the doubt that I could get though it gracefully. The Approach happened as the accidents got fewer and farther between and she had the little victories of staying dry at naptime and even overnight most nights.

We had some Ordeals through the process. For example, on a road trip, we stopped to take a potty break and Ember absolutely refused to go. There were threats and bribes and yelling. It was not pretty, and all of us died a little that day, but the lessons that came from the experience were invaluable. I faced my fears and slayed my dragon when I learned to let go and trust that she knows her body better than I do and that I can't force her to go. She learned that persistence wins. The Rewards were plentiful. Ember gained confidence and more autonomy. I no longer have to bring diapers and wipes with me, and of course, I never have to change a poopy diaper again! The Road Back was sharing our experience with other parents going through the same thing and what we learned in the process. I was Resurrected as a more laid-back parent who no longer had a diaper bag and could feel free to walk out of the house more easily.

Our Children Are on Their Own Journeys

Letting go is one of the hardest parts of parenting. As our kids grow up and become more independent, we have to realize that they are going to have journeys without us, and we should allow them that opportunity. We grow the most when we fail, so we should let our children stumble often to allow learning to occur for them. When our kids are tested, it's great to be their allies, but we need to allow them to be the heroes of their own stories. When your son forgets his backpack at home, he will face some challenges at school that day, but by coming to his rescue, what do we teach him? We teach him that he doesn't need to be responsible himself because we will fix his problems. When we are the heroes all the time, they become dependent on us and don't learn to do things for themselves.

We need to be the heroes of our own stories and not live vicariously or try to be our kid's heroes. Our big role in their lives is to be their support system. We need to be on their side and validate their feelings. We need to share personal lessons learned from our own journeys, but not dictate theirs. We need to let them fully experience their journey to gain the lessons to lead them into their adult lives. Our job as parents is not to shelter them from the world but help them develop the skills they will need to be an active participant in it. We need to give them the space to have their own unique experiences and then bring their stories back to the village. We also need to be at home when they return to tell of their adventures and willingly listen to their tales. As Campbell said, "Follow your bliss," and I'd add, allow your children the opportunity to find their own.

Final Thoughts on Perspective

Parenting gives you opportunities every day to fail, to make amends, and to change your approach to do better next time. Our kids become our mirrors to help us create the changes we want to see in them first for ourselves. We need to encourage our kids to be their own heroes and learn from their unique experiences. Our love for them pushes us to be better versions of ourselves, which in turn, gives them the freedom to become the best version of themselves. In the words of Master Shifu in Kung Fu Panda 3, "I'm not trying to teach you to be me; I'm trying to teach you to be you."

Mike and I are big believers in the idea that everything that happens in our lives is there to teach us something. As a reader of this book, you are clearly dedicated to learning. The secret is to learn not only through reading, seminars, podcasts, mentors, and coaches, but from everything that happens in your life. As our friend Matt Aitchison says, "I'm a student of life, and I'm always looking for my next teacher." This is a healthy perspective to have when it comes to living life to the fullest and becoming the best parent you can be.

PARENTING PROFILE

David Osborn

David is an entrepreneur, public speaker, and author. He is also the principal owner of Keller Williams Realty, the 19th largest real estate company in the US, which grossed over $5.2 billion in sales last year.

David is a father of two daughters, ages 6 and 28. He and his wife, Traci, live in Austin, Texas.

Parenting Philosophy

The responsibility of raising a child is high, but ultimately, I think our job is simply to hold space for the child to become whoever the child needs to become. Even though I feel responsibility and burden, I also realize that I'm not really in charge of her destiny. I'm here to be in charge of her nourishment while she grows and to be a support for her. Instead of asking questions that lead to the outcome I want, I ask open questions. How was your day? What did you enjoy doing? What do you love about that? I don't steer things in any particular direction. I just hold a space of love and curiosity and then create that framework for her to grow into whatever she needs to be.

How has the Miracle Morning affected your parenting?

I think the visualizations and the affirmations are two things that I was aware of, but hadn't been using a lot before I started practicing the Miracle Morning. I visualize my family having a tremendously warm and loving family environment and getting time together. Sure enough, as happens in life, the more I visualize that, the more I affirm it, and the more it becomes true.

Best Parenting Tips

Take care of your health. I'm an older parent, so I want to be around for a long time for my kids. I want to be healthy for them, so I eat differently than I used to. I work out differently than I used to. Everything I do now is focused on what would create longevity for me and therefore enable me to stick around longer for my kids. I'm probably in better shape now in my late forties than I was in my late thirties, and a lot of that has to do with the change in my focus.

Be careful of perfectionism. My experience of being a parent is one of constantly questioning myself if I did something right or wrong. Could I have done it better? The awareness that I did something wrong shows my desire to be a great parent. So I show gratitude toward that part of me, but I don't listen to the part of me that wants to worry and finagle things to death. Perfectionism is a habit, like biting your nails. Once you're aware that you don't want to bite your nails anymore, you just stop biting them.

Like anything in life, fortunately I'm very comfortable with self-doubt because I'm an entrepreneur, and I've been living off my own wits for a long time.

Pay attention to diet. We're really attentive to what we eat. As most parents know, it's not easy to get kids to eat healthy foods. We've had some wins; we've had some losses. Our daughter will eat pumpkin or sunflower seeds, and she loves fruit. Those are wins for us.

Play catch with your child. I read an article when my daughter was first born that said the difference between hand-eye coordination in sports is almost everything. If you'll just do five minutes of ball sport with your kid every day, whether it's rolling a ball along the ground or playing catch, you'll train their hand-eye coordination to a high level.

Keep things in perspective. I used to have a sign on my garage wall. It was a whiteboard, and I wrote on it, "Think eternal." I ask myself, what's going to happen in a thousand years? What is the impact we're having, of our actions now, on the world a thousand years from now? If you think that way, you can't be worried about any of the small stuff because none of it matters. Raising children who care about the world, are responsible people, have integrity, and good moral character is the best thing you can leave behind. Thinking about your mortality helps put everything in perspective.

Be aware that life's very short. We come from dust, and we go to dust, and I remind myself of that constantly. I think by realizing that the timeline you have on Earth is getting shorter, whatever it is, whenever the end is, makes you not want to waste any time on silly anxiety, wasteful activities, or behaviors, and being anxious is a wasteful behavior. I need to be fully present to whatever my goals and missions are, and being a dad is one of them. I don't serve my child by having anxiety over serving my child.

Final Word

Awareness is huge. It works on so many levels in life. That's where it all begins, just having a willingness. Waking up in the morning and going through your morning ritual, your Miracle Morning, and asking yourself, What do I need to be aware of today? Where am I on track, where am I not on track, and what affirmations would help me be a better father?

PARENTING PROFILE
Traci Osborn

Traci is a stay-at-home mom. She lives in Austin, Texas, with her husband David and has one daughter, age 6.

How has parenting affected your life?

I think parenting is a great teacher of compassion. Being a parent has taught me a deeper type of love, a deeper understanding of people in general, their circumstances, and what they're going through.

Best Parenting Tips

Failure is how you learn. As parents, we need to change our perspective on failure. I think it's inevitable to beat yourself up, because you care so much about your relationship with your kids. Ultimately they depend on you—for everything. How do you stop beating yourself up? Just remember that you're a human being and you make mistakes, and when you fail, you can't let it beat you down. You can't because, otherwise, you don't grow and you don't move. You can't move on from that, and that doesn't do anyone good.

Don't tell your child to "be careful." I have to remind myself not to say, "Be careful" to my daughter all the time. I want her to make her own mistakes. If something happens and she cries, then that's just something that she will learn from, she'll gain insight from, rather than her mom or dad constantly stepping in to solve her problems.

Use "be aware" instead. The one phrase I learned was, "Be aware of your body." That doesn't tell them that the world is a frightening place and you have to be careful. It just means, "Be aware of what's happening. You could fall. Do you want to take that risk? If you do, go for it." Then they can decide, "This is okay for me to take this risk," or "No, this is not okay for me to take this risk."

Re-evaluate. I think good parenting involves constantly thinking, analyzing, and asking, "Is this still good for her?" Maybe it's not. Maybe next year it won't be a good fit for her. So be willing to change your approach if you find it's no longer working.

Self-care is important. I go work out to relieve stress. I take time for myself. I think if you don't do that, you get burned out. I try and remember that I'm doing the best I can. There's nothing more you can do than the best that you can do.

Give your kids a voice. Just to have a voice when you're a kid, to be able to voice your opinion, is a huge thing. Later on, you won't have to be rebellious because you've always had a voice. It used to be that, if you did speak your mind, then you were the bad kid or you were rebellious. Now, it's okay. Parents can say, what is your opinion? Tell me what you think. Let's work something out. I just love that because kids can teach us so much, as much as we can teach them.

Parenting Success Story

Like many parents, I used to yell a lot. That's not something I'm very proud of, but it's just probably a learned behavior from when I was a kid. When I was a kid, the thing was to behave well. But if you want good behavior, yelling doesn't help. I had to stop, look, and analyze, and even now, when I'm frustrated or in a hurry, I want to trigger back to that behavior. It's something I am still working on. Any success in your life, be it parenting, or a job, or a relationship, actually takes failure. Parenting is one of those skills that requires you to fail and learn from it. Through those failures, you will gain success.

Final Word

A message to moms: I think moms have a really hard time more so than men. Moms feel a humongous responsibility, and they put a lot of pressure on themselves. They don't take time for themselves. I think that's a huge mistake. I think you have to take time for yourself to be a better person, to recharge. If you don't, you get so drained, you don't remember that you're your own person and you aren't just a structure for your children or your family. You have your own needs and wants. That's probably one of the most important things in parenting, to remember that you need time, you need space to be a better parent and to be a better partner.

— 10 —
THE MIRACLE EQUATION
Bonus Chapter by Hal Elrod

*For those who are willing to make an effort, great miracles
and wonderful treasures are in store.*
—Isaac Bashevis Singer, Author and Nobel Prize Winner

You understand now that you *can* wake up early, maintain extraordinary levels of energy, direct your focus, and master the not-so-obvious parenting success skills from Lindsay and Mike. If you also apply what follows to your parenting, you're going to go much further: you're going to make your parenting truly exceptional.

To make this leap, there is one more helpful tool for you to add to your parenting toolbox, and it's called The Miracle Equation.

The Miracle Equation is the underlying strategy that I used to realize my full potential as a salesperson, and as a parent. And it has to do with how you handle your goals. One of my mentors, Dan Casetta, taught me: "The purpose of a goal isn't to hit the goal. The real purpose is to develop yourself into the type of person who can achieve your goals, regardless of whether you hit that particular one or not. It is who you become by giving it everything you have until the last moment—regardless of your results—that matters most."

When you make the decision to stick with a seemingly unachievable goal, despite the fact that the possibility of failure is high, you will become especially focused, faithful, and intentional. When your objective is truly ambitious, it will actually require you to find out what you are really made of!

Two Decisions

As with any great challenge, you need to make decisions related to achieving the goal. You can set a deadline and then create your own agenda by asking yourself, "If I were to achieve my goal on the deadline, what decisions would I have to make and commit to in advance?"

And you'll find that whatever the goal, the two decisions that would make the biggest impact are *always the same*. They form the basis for The Miracle Equation.

The First Decision: Unwavering Faith

There was a time in my life when I was trying to achieve an impossible sales goal. I'll use that as an example to show you what I mean. Though this comes from my sales experience, I'll show you how it applies within the context of parenting (or any context, really). It was a stressful time, and I was already facing fear and self-doubt, but my thought process about the goal forced me to an important realization. To achieve the seemingly impossible, I would have to maintain unwavering faith every day, *regardless of my results*.

I knew that there would be moments when I would doubt myself and times when I would be so far off track that the goal would no longer seem achievable. But it would be those moments when I would have to override self-doubt with unshakeable faith.

To keep that level of faith in those challenging moments, I repeated what I call my Miracle Mantra:

I will _____ (reach my goal), no matter what. There is no other option.

Understand that maintaining unwavering faith isn't *normal*. It's not what most people do. When it doesn't look like the desired result is likely, average performers give up the faith that it's possible. When the game is on the line, a team is down on the scorecards, and there are only seconds left, it is only the top performers—the Michael Jordans of the world—who, without hesitation, tell their team, "Give me the ball."

The rest of the team breathes a sigh of relief because of their fear of missing the game-winning shot, while Michael Jordan made a decision at some point in his life that he would maintain unwavering faith, despite the fact that he might miss. (And although Michael Jordan missed 26 game-winning shots in his career, his faith that he would make every single one never wavered.)

That's the first decision that very successful people make, and it's yours for the making, too.

When you're working toward a goal and you're not on track, what is the first thing that goes out the window? *The faith that the outcome you want is possible.* Your self-talk turns negative: *I'm not on track. It doesn't look like I'm going to reach my goal.* And with each passing moment, your faith decreases.

You don't have to settle for that. You have the ability and the choice to maintain that same unwavering faith, no matter what, and regardless of the results. This is key in parenting because results are often out of your direct control. You may doubt yourself or have a bad day with the kids. In the darkest moments, you wonder if everything will turn out okay. But you must find—over and over again—your faith that all things are possible and hold it throughout your journey, whether it is a 30-day toilet training goal or a 30-year parenting career.

It's very important that you see your role as a parent as directly related to other high-achieving professions, because the parallels are unmistakable. If you don't take time to see the parallels here, you may find that you focus on the failures of your parenting instead of the successes. And if you focus on the failures, your kids will too, and that's not what you want. So stay with me.

Elite athletes maintain unwavering faith that they can make every shot they take. That faith—and the faith you need to develop—isn't based on probability. It comes from a whole different place. Most salespeople operate based on what is known as the *law of averages.*

But what we're talking about here is the *law of miracles*. When you miss shot after shot you have to tell yourself what Michael Jordan tells himself, *I've missed three, but I want the ball next, and I'm going to make that next shot.*

And if you miss that one, *your faith doesn't waiver*. You repeat the Miracle Mantra to yourself:

I will _____ (reach my goal), no matter what. There is no other option.

Then, you simply uphold your integrity and do what it is that you say you are going to do.

An elite athlete may be having the worst game ever, where it seems like in the first three-quarters of the game, they can't make a shot to save their life. Yet in the fourth quarter, right when the team needs them, they start making those shots. They always want the ball; they always have belief and faith in themselves. In the fourth quarter, they score three times as many shots as they've made in the first three-quarters of the game.

Why? They have conditioned themselves to have unwavering faith in their talents, skills, and abilities, regardless of what it says on the scoreboard or their stats sheet.

And ...

They combine their unwavering faith with part two of The Miracle Equation: extraordinary effort.

The Second Decision: Extraordinary Effort

When you allow your faith to go out the window, effort almost always follows right behind it. *After all*, you tell yourself, *what's the point in even trying to achieve your goal if it's not possible?* Suddenly, you find yourself wondering how you're ever going to teach your child to read or to be polite or to study, let alone reach the big goal you've been working toward.

I've been there many times, feeling deflated, thinking, *what's the point of even trying?* And you might easily think, *There's no way I can make it. My kids are headed in the wrong direction.*

That's where extraordinary effort comes into play. You need to stay focused on your original goal—you need to connect to the vision you had for it, that big *why* in your heart and mind when you set the goal in the first place.

Like me, you need to reverse engineer the goal. Ask yourself, *If I'm at the end of this month and this goal were to have happened, what would I have done? What would I have needed to do?*

Whatever the answer, you will need to stay consistent and persevere, regardless of your results. You have to believe you can still ring the bell of success at the end. You have to maintain unwavering faith and extraordinary effort—until the buzzer sounds. That's the only way that you create an opportunity for the miracle to happen.

As parents, our extraordinary effort is to model the behavior we want and to create the environment that will enable our kids to grow. We encourage and support and motivate our children. We do not use force. Force always backfires. We provide the structure and let the children have free choice within it.

If you do what the average person does—what our built-in human nature tells us to do—you'll be just like every other average parent. Don't choose to be that average person! Remember: your thoughts and actions create your results and are therefore a self-fulfilling prophecy. So manage them wisely.

Allow me to introduce you to your edge—the strategy that will practically ensure every one of your goals is realized.

The Miracle Equation

Unwavering Faith + Extraordinary Effort = Miracles

It's easier than you think. The secret to maintaining unwavering faith is to recognize that it's a mindset and a *strategy*—it's not concrete. In fact, it's elusive. You can never make *every* sale. No athlete makes *every* shot. You can never win every battle as a parent. So, you have to program yourself automatically to have the unwavering faith to drive you to keep putting forth the extraordinary effort—regardless of the results.

Remember, the key to putting this equation into practice, to maintaining unwavering faith in the midst of self-doubt, is the Miracle Mantra:

I will _____, no matter what. There is no other option.

Once you set a goal, put that goal into the Miracle Mantra format. Yes, you're going to say your affirmations every morning (and maybe every evening, too). But all day, every day, you're going to repeat your Miracle Mantra to yourself. As you're driving the kids to school or taking the train to the office, while you're on the treadmill, in the shower, in line at the grocery store—in other words: *everywhere you go.*

Your Miracle Mantra will fortify your faith and be the self-talk you need to make just one more try, try after try.

Bonus Lesson

Remember what I learned from my mentor Dan Casetta on the purpose of goals. You have to become the type of person who *can* achieve the goal. You won't always reach the goal, but you can become someone who maintains unwavering faith and puts forth extraordinary effort, regardless of your results. That's how you become the type of person you need to become to achieve extraordinary goals consistently. What a great lesson for your children!

And while reaching the goal almost doesn't matter (almost!), more often than not, you'll reach your goal. Do the elite athletes win every time? No. But they win most of the time. And you'll win most of the time, too.

At the end of the day, you can wake up earlier, do the Life S.A.V.E.R.S. with passion and excitement, get organized, focused, and intentional, and master every parenting challenge like a champ. And yet, if you don't combine unwavering faith with extraordinary effort, you won't reach the levels of success you seek.

The Miracle Equation gives you access to forces outside of anyone's understanding, using an energy that I might call God, the Universe, the Law of Attraction, or even good luck. I don't know how it works; I just know that it works.

You've read this far—you clearly want success more than almost anything. Commit to following through with every aspect of parenting, including The Miracle Equation. You deserve it, and I want you to have it!

Putting It into Action:

1. Write out the Miracle Equation and put it where you will see it every day: **Unwavering Faith + Extraordinary Effort = Miracles (UF + EE = M∞)**

2. What's your number one goal for your parenting journey this year? What goal, if you were to accomplish it, would bring you closest to your ideal family life?

3. Write your Miracle Mantra: *I will _____ (insert your goals and daily actions, here), no matter what. There is no other option.*

It is more about who you become in the process. You'll expand your self-confidence and, regardless of your results, the very next time you attempt to reach a goal, and every time after that, you'll be the type of person who gives it all they've got.

Closing Remarks

Congratulations! You have done what only a small percentage of people do: read an entire book. If you've come this far, that tells me something about you: you have a thirst for more. You want to become more, do more, contribute more, and earn more.

Right now, you have the unprecedented opportunity to infuse the Life S.A.V.E.R.S. into your daily life and business, upgrade your daily routine, and ultimately upgrade your *life* to a first class experience beyond your wildest dreams. Before you know it, you will be reaping the astronomical benefits of the habits that top achievers use daily.

Five years from now, your family life, business, relationships, and income will be a direct result of one thing: *who you've become.* It's up to you to wake up each day and dedicate time to becoming the best version of yourself. Seize this moment in time, define a vision for your future, and use what you've learned in this book to turn your vision into your reality.

Imagine a time just a few years from now when you come across the journal you started after completing this book. In it, you find the goals you wrote down for yourself—dreams you didn't dare speak out loud at the time. And as you look around, you realize *your dreams now represent the life you are living.*

Right now, you stand at the foot of a mountain you can easily and effortlessly climb. All you need to do is continue waking up each day for your Miracle Morning and use the Life S.A.V.E.R.S. day after day, month after month, year after year, as you continue to take your *self,* your *family,* and your *success* to levels beyond what you've ever experienced before.

Combine your Miracle Morning with a commitment to master your Skills for Exceptional Parents and use The Miracle Equation to create results that most people only dream of.

This book was written as an expression of what we know will work for you, to take every area of your life to the next level, faster than you may currently believe is possible. Miraculous performers weren't born that way—they have simply dedicated their lives to developing themselves and their skills to achieve everything they've ever wanted.

You can become one of them, I promise.

Taking Action: The 30-Day Miracle Morning Challenge

Now it is time to join the tens of thousands of people who have transformed their lives with *The Miracle Morning.* Join the community online at TMMBook.com and download the toolkit to get you started *today.*

ABOUT THE AUTHORS

HAL ELROD is one of the highest rated keynote speakers in America, but is best known as the author of what is now being widely regarded as "one of the most life-changing books ever written" (and is quickly becoming one of the highest rated books on Amazon, with over 1,500 five-star reviews), The Miracle Morning: The Not-So-Obvious Secret Guaranteed To Transform Your Life ... (Before 8AM). Hal died at age 20. Hit head-on by a drunk driver at 70 miles per hour, he broke 11 bones, was clinically dead for six minutes, spent six days in a coma, and was told he would never walk again. Defying the logic of doctors and the temptations to be a victim, Hal went on to not only walk but to run a 52-mile ultramarathon, become a hall of fame business achiever, an international keynote speaker, host of one of the top success podcasts on iTunes called Achieve Your Goals with Hal Elrod, and most importantly ... he is grateful to be alive and living the life of his dreams with his wife, Ursula, and their two children, Sophie and Halsten. For more information on Hal's speaking, writing, and coaching, please visit HalElrod.com.

LINDSAY AND MIKE MCCARTHY. Mike was born in Colorado and graduated with his BA in business from the University of Colorado. Lindsay grew up in Pennsylvania and was a student athlete at James Madison University before she married Mike and they started building their lives together. Mike and Lindsay have been married since 2006 and have two amazing children, Tyler and Ember. Mike is a serial entrepreneur who is the Regional Owner for the Greater Pennsylvania region of Keller Williams Realty, the CEO of a men's adventure mastermind group called GoBundance, a certified Spirit Coach ™, co-owner of Tomoka Brewing Company as well as an avid real estate investor. Lindsay worked with Mike on the Keller Williams

Greater Pennsylvania regional team, but always dreamed to be a stay-at-home mom, so when Tyler came along she put her full energy into that role. Lindsay is also a certified Spirit Led Practitioner™. Mike and Lindsay are also the creators of GratefulParent.com and are so excited to add author to their bios since it has been an aspiration of theirs for a long time. The McCarthy's are an adventurous homeschool family living in Pennsylvania, but love to travel as much as possible and share new experiences.

HONORÉE CORDER is the author of 20 books, including *You Must Write a Book*, *Vision to Reality*, *Prosperity for Writers*, *Business Dating*, The Successful Single Mom Book Series, *If Divorce is a Game*, and *The Divorced Phoenix*. She is also Hal Elrod's business partner in The Miracle Morning Book Series. She coaches business professionals, writers, and aspiring non-fiction authors who want to publish their books to bestseller status, create a platform, and develop multiple streams of income. **Learn more at HonoreeCorder.com.**

A Special Invitation from Hal

Fans and readers of *The Miracle Morning* make up an extraordinary community of like-minded individuals who wake up each day dedicated to fulfilling the unlimited potential that is within all of us. As the author of *The Miracle Morning*, it was my desire to create an online space where readers and fans could go to connect, get encouragement, share best practices, support one another, discuss the book, post videos, find an accountability partner, and even swap smoothie recipes and exercise routines.

I honestly had no idea that The Miracle Morning Community would become one of the most inspiring, engaged, and supportive online communities in the world, but it has. I'm blown away by the caliber of our 40,000+ members, which consists of people from all around the globe and is growing daily.

Just go to **www.MyTMMCommunity.com** and request to join The Miracle Morning Community (on Facebook). Here you'll be able to connect with others who are already practicing The Miracle Morning—many of whom have been doing it for years—to get additional support and accelerate your success. I'll be moderating the community and checking in regularly. I look forward to seeing you there!

If you'd like to connect with me personally on social media, follow **@HalElrod** on Twitter and **Facebook.com/YoPalHal** on Facebook. Please feel free to send me a direct message, leave a comment, or ask me a question. I do my best to answer every single one, so let's connect soon!

BOOK HAL TO SPEAK!

Book Hal As Your Keynote Speaker and You're Guaranteed to Make Your Event Highly Enjoyable & Unforgettable!

For more than a decade, Hal Elrod has been consistently rated as the #1 Keynote Speaker by meeting planners and attendees. His unique style combines inspiring audiences with his unbelieveable TRUE story, keeping them laughing hysterically with his high energy, stand-up comedy style delivery, and empowering them with actionable strategies to take their RESULTS to the next level.

"Hal received a 9.8 out of 10 from our members. That never happens." –**Entrepreneur Organization (NYC Chapter)**

"Hal was the featured keynote speaker for 400 of our top sales performers and executive team. He gave us a plan that was so simple, we had no choice but to put it into action immediately." –**Art Van Furniture**

"Bringing Hal in to be the keynote speaker at our annual conference was the best investment we could have made." –**Fidelity National Title**

For More Info - Visit www.HalElrod.com

THE MIRACLE MORNING SERIES

The JOURNAL

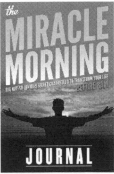

For Writers

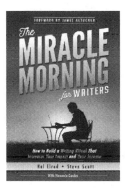

For Real Estate Agents

For Salespeople

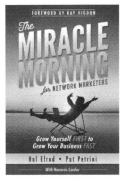

For Network Marketers

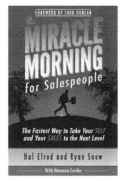

COMING SOON...

The Miracle Morning for Entrepreneurs

The Miracle Morning for Transforming Your Relationship

The Miracle Morning for College Students

Made in the USA
San Bernardino, CA
25 September 2016